Krakow

A CITY GUIDE

by
Dorota Wąsik
and
Emma Roper-Evans

SOMERSET LIMITED

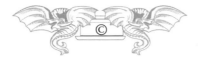

Vörösmarty tér 1, Pf. 71
1051 Budapest, Hungary
Felelős kiadó: Ruszin Zsolt, a Somerset Kft. igazgatója
office@visiblecities.net
www.visiblecities.net
Visible Cities is a registered trademark.

Layout & Design: *Regina Rácz*
Photographs: *Sebastian Stachowski*
Diagrams: *Imre Bába*
Architectural Drawings: *Michael Mansell RIBA*
Maps: *Dimap Bt.*
Repro Studio: *Overprint Kft.*
Printed by: *Novoprint Rt. Attila Miseje, Director*

Acknowledgements:
*With special thanks to Scott Simpson, Ildikó Baumgartner, Anna Bubula,
Anne-Maree Byworth, Zoltán Dénes, Dóra Herceg, Dorota Leśniak-
Rychlak, Paula Lodzinska, Mónika Papp, George Semler, Michał Skiba,
Marta Slusarczyk, Silvia Svejenova, Sylwia Trzaska, Fiona van Haeringen.*

This is the first edition of Visible Cities Krakow:
corrections and general comments will be welcomed.

Other titles in the Visible Cities series:
Visible Cities Budapest (2nd edition)
Visible Cities Dubrovnik
Visible Cities Vienna (October 2002)
Further titles are in preparation.

Series Editor: Annabel Barber

Cover illustration: *Detail from the Veit Stoss altar in St Mary's (1477).*
Cover Photo: *Paweł Pencakowski*
Previous page: *Dragon detail from a building by Teodor Talowski.*

Cracovian by birth, education and choice, **Dorota Wąsik** has been studying
the city's history for over ten years. She has produced film documentaries,
and published art, architecture and travel articles. **Emma Roper-Evans** is a
writer, translator and journalist based in Budapest, Hungary. She is co-
author of Visible Cities Budapest, and has published articles in British
newspapers on the Krakow Jewish Festival.

ISBN 963 00 5930 4

5

CONTENTS

INTRODUCTION

There have always been dragons in Krakow. The first-recorded of them harassed and ate the subjects of the legendary King Krak. It emerged from a lair under Wawel Hill to seize its prey until killed by Skuba, a wily shoemaker, who managed to decoy the beast with a sheep's carcass stuffed with sulphur and tar. The dragon ate the lot, and then rushed to the Vistula River to quench his sudden raging thirst. He drank and drank, sucking up the river water until he eventually burst in a spectacular cloud of scales, sheep bits and tar.

Since then dragons have appeared in various forms throughout Krakow's history. The city was raided by the Tartars; the Swedish, Russian and Austrian armies marched through it; the Nazi governor Hans Frank resided in Wawel Castle, and the chimneys of the Nowa Huta steelworks emitted invisible poison that blemished the faces of ancient monuments: and yet, in spite of all these assaults, Krakow survived. The dragons were slain, the armies were conquered, and the city lives on after a thousand years. Some say that this is due to its *chakhra*, a mystic stone which radiates energy from Wawel Hill. Who knows? But *chakhra* or not, the city undoubtedly contains a wealth of works of art and architecture. It boasts some 150 churches, ancient synagogues, some true Gothic and Renaissance masterpieces, and the biggest mediæval square in Europe, still the vital centre of the city's life.

Home to one of the oldest universities in Europe, the Jagiellonian University (established in 1364), the city has educated and inspired figures as diverse as Copernicus and Pope John Paul II, the Nobel Prize-winning poets Czesław Miłosz and Wisława Szymborska, writers Stanisław Lem and Sławomir Mrożek, theatre and film directors such as Tadeusz Kantor and Andrzej Wajda, the painter Stanisław Wyspiański and composer Krzysztof Penderecki.

At the beginning of the 17th century, King Zygmunt Vasa moved his capital from Krakow to Warsaw, but Cracovians still believe that their city reigns supreme.

ul. Floriańska, one of the major streets of Krakow's Old Town, leading from the Rynek Market Square to the mediæval St Florian's Gate.

The Sukiennice (Cloth Hall) in the Rynek Market Square, with cobblestones glistening after the rain.

PRONUNCIATION

Polish is a Slavic language that uses the Roman alphabet, "customised" with some diacritics:

c:	"ts": like the "ts" in Betsy.
cz:	like the "ch" in church.
ł:	like the "w" in weary.
ó (or u):	pronounced like "oo" in moon, but shorter.
sz:	like the "sh" in hash.
w:	like the "v" in visit.
ż (or rz):	like the "ge" in bourgeois.
ą and ę:	nasal vowels, adding an "n" sound after them.
ń:	like the "ny" in news.
ś and ź:	soft "sh" and "zh" as in action and pleasure.

HOW TO USE THIS GUIDE

This book is organised into five sections. Part I contains the history of Krakow. Part II consists of the main guidebook chapters on what to do and see in the city itself, concentrating on art, architecture and music as subjects for which Krakow is particularly celebrated. Part III comprises four short guided walks around the old town and just outside it. Each walk is planned to take about an hour, and is marked on an accompanying map. Part IV contains a short selection of day trips further afield. Part V covers food and wine, gives practical tips about the town, and includes a short, selective list of restaurants, hotels, cafés and bars.

STANISLAUS OF KRAKOW (1010-1079)

Stanislaus, patron saint of Poland and of Krakow (*see picture on following page*), began his career as a canon in Krakow cathedral, from where he advanced to the position of Bishop in 1072. He was generous to the poor, but madly zealous in his desire for reform, which enraged many of the nobles, including the king, Bolesław the Bold. When Bolesław abducted the wife of another man and smuggled her into his palace, Stanislaus rebuked him severely, and ordered that mass was to be suspended as soon as the king so much as set foot in the cathedral. Bolesław vowed to have his revenge, and ordered his retainers to kill the bishop. When they demurred, Bolesław is said to have unsheathed his own sword and done the deed himself, hacking off Stanislaus' head and flinging his body into a pond beside the Skałka Church (*see p. 74*). Pope Gregory VII instantly confirmed his excommunication, and refused to have anything more to do with Poland. Stanislaus was canonised in the mid 13th century. His relics are housed in Wawel Cathedral (*see p. 23*), and every year on 8th May a ceremonial procession takes them through the town to the church of St Michael on Skałka, the scene of his murder.

HISTORY

The white rock of Wawel Hill, rising above the Jurassic plain overlooking the River Vistula's fens and marshes, formed a natural defensive site from pre-historic times. Neolithic tribes were the first to settle here, and the region has been continuously inhabited ever since.

Krakow straddled the crossroads of important east-west and north-south trade routes, and maintained a lively commercial relationship with the Roman Empire. It became a key point along the famous Amber Trail, a Roman trading route from where the Vistula meets the Baltic, source of the amber, and running right down the continent to the Adriatic Sea, and thence back to Rome.

In the mid 10th century Duke Mieszko I converted to Christianity, the new religion, which had most probably been introduced by Bohemian missionaries. As elsewhere in the region, the decision to convert was born as much of pragmatism as of religious conviction, the aim being to unite Krakow with the developing western Church, and form a bulwark against German tribal aggression. It is from around this time (AD 965) that the name Krakow first appears, in the writings of a Sephardic merchant from Cordoba, Ibrahim Ibn Yaqub, who came here to buy salt, copper, silver and other goods produced in the Duchy of Małopolska, of which Krakow was the capital.

By the end of the first millennium, the bishopric of Krakow had been founded, and the town comprised a Romanesque cathedral, a castle and a citadel surrounded by ramparts, all built on Wawel Hill. In the first half of the 11th century, Krakow officially became the capital of the kingdom, under Kazimierz the Restorer (1038-1058), of the Piast dynasty. His successor, Bolesław II (1058-1079), was a strong - even headstrong - ruler (*see p. 9*), determined to make his kingdom a counterpoise to the growing might of the Germano-centric Holy Roman Empire.

In 1241 came the first of a series of Tartar invasions. The country was never completely overrun, but much was destroyed. German settlers were called in to clear the land and colonise new areas, and the result was a burgeoning of agri-culture, trade and culture. Krakow rose phoenix-like from its own ashes. In 1257 it received its town charter, and proceeded to draft and execute the urban

St Stanislaus of Kraków, bishop and martyr (see p. 9), patron saint of Poland and Kraków.

Genealogy of the Jagiellonian dynasty, who ruled Poland in the 15th and 16th centuries.

plan that has survived to this day. To keep the Tartars at bay once and for all, a system of city ramparts and fortifications was erected. The 14th century was Krakow's first golden age, under its ruler Kazimierz the Great (1333-1370), the monarch who "inherited a Poland made of wood, and left behind him a country of solid brick". The school he founded in 1364 became a university in 1400 and, as the Jagiellonian University, went on to become one of the major intellectual centres in Central and Eastern Europe. A great legislator and promoter of trade and learning, Kazimierz turned mediæval Krakow into a flourishing capital, founding two more fortified towns beside it, which is why early engravings of Krakow show three cities, Cracovia, Casimirus and Clepardia. The town of Kazimierz was surrounded by its own walls and separated by an old arm of the Vistula River (now dried up). King Kazimierz had no direct heir, and when he died the throne passed to Ludwik (Lajos) of Hungary, who paid scant attention to the country but ruled through regents. Lajos had a daughter, however, Jadwiga, and when Lajos died Jadwiga - still a little girl - was elected to rule, and crowned the official "King of Poland" in 1382. In 1386, at the age of 12, she married Władysław Jagiello, Grand Duke of Lithuania, thus effecting a union between the Kingdom of Poland and the Duchy of Lithuania, a union which made Poland the largest kingdom in Europe. Large it may have been - but not large enough: it still lacked an outlet to the Baltic, and Władysław's reign was taken up with battles against the Teutonic Knights, who controlled the coastal region. By the 16th century the territory had been won, and King Stefan Batory (1575-1586) forged a Polish-Lithuanian-Swedish alliance aimed specifically at controlling the Baltic coast.

The Jagiellonian dynasty was connected by marriage to many of the royal families of Europe, including the houses of Habsburg (Spain and Austria), Hohenzollern (Prussia), and Vasa (Sweden). It was under these rulers that Krakow really began to flourish. This was also the time of the rise of the gentry and merchant classes, a trend which increased to such an extent, in fact, that in 1572 Poland became a Royal Republic, with a king elected by Parliament as titular head of the realm.

The transfer of the Polish capital to Warsaw in 1609, by King Zygmunt Vasa, marked the beginning of the city's decline. Throughout the 17th century the rise of the Polish gentry had continued unabated, culminating in their so-called "Golden Freedom", a system of semi-democracy which unfortunately evolved – or rather degenerated – into anarchy. In 1655 the country suffered a Swedish invasion - referred to by Poles as the "deluge", which escalated into two Swedish wars (1655-60 and 1703-21). The seeds of ultimate disintegration were sown. In the 18th century, Poland was gradually partitioned and annexed by its neighbours: Russia, Prussia and Austria. The Polish struggle for freedom was valiant and heartstrong, but doomed to failure, personified in the

Painting of the 1850 Fire of Krakow, showing the Dominican Monastery in flames.

romantic figure of Tadeusz Kościuszko (*see p. 48*), who, after the second partition, when Krakow was occupied by the Russians, attempted to preserve what remained of Polish sovereignty. On 24th March 1794, in Krakow's Market Square (Rynek), Kościuszko proclaimed a National Insurrection and vowed to serve the cause as the leader of a revolutionary government. The spot where he swore his famous oath (near the Town Hall Tower) is commemorated with a marble plaque.

In 1795, despite the fact that Kościuszko and his men had had their swords blessed in the Loreto Chapel of the Capuchin Church, Krakow fell to the Austrians. At the Treaty of St Petersburg in 1797, Austria, Russia and Prussia met to ratify their separate claims on the parts of Poland they had taken as their share, and agreed that the name Poland should officially cease to be used.

For the next 20 years Krakow existed as a provincial outpost of the vast Austro-Hungarian empire. After the fall of Napoleon, however, when Europe's borders were redrawn at the Congress of Vienna (1815), the Republic of Krakow was created, giving the city a little more autonomy. This quasi-free status was lost three decades later, after the Krakow Uprising of 1846, when the city rose against its Habsburg overlords. The uprising was crushed, and Vienna reacted by revoking Krakow's free status. In 1866, however, Austria suffered a military defeat at the hands of Prussia. Alarmed at this show of enemy might on his own doorstep, the emperor Franz Joseph deemed it expedient to be more conciliatory towards his subject peoples. In 1867, the same year that Austria accorded Hungary new powers within the empire, the province of Galicia ("Austrian Poland", populated mainly by Poles and Ruthenians, with its capital at Lemberg, now Lviv, Ukraine) was given wide-ranging autonomy by the Habsburgs, and Polish language and culture were allowed to develop freely.

Though Krakow is not officially a part of Galicia, the city was certainly affected by the new freedoms, and was heavily influenced by Lemberg - there was a constant flux of people and ideas between the two cities. By the turn of the 19th century a new sense of cultural identity was flourishing. Krakow became Poland's nucleus of national pride and fanned its independent spirit. The last of a series of national uprisings succeeded in restoring Poland's sovereignty in 1918, when the Austro-Hungarian empire collapsed after World War I. Both the fight for independence, and the new Polish state, re-established after 123 years of occupation, were led by Marshal Józef Piłsudski. His tomb is now in the Wawel crypt.

15th-century map of Krakow showing the two towns of Cracovia and Casimirus, separated by an arm of the Vistula which has since dried up.

Unlike many other Polish cities, Krakow was spared the physical destruction of World War II. The intellectual and cultural toll on the city was immense, however, and the city's Jewish community, which had enriched cultural and commercial life since the middle ages, was exterminated by the Nazis. The war either claimed the lives or displaced nearly all of the 70,000 Jews who lived in Krakow before 1939.

Communism (or "Real Socialism" as it was mockingly termed) also left its mark on Krakow. The town received the unwelcome gift of a steel industry and the steelworkers' town of Nowa Huta (New Foundry), a creation of socialist propaganda, designed as a model workers' town to counterbalance the ideologically undesirable intellectual and bourgeois elements of the city. When the gigantic statue of Lenin, which had towered over Nowa Huta since its establishment, was finally removed, people saw it as a sure sign that the unsuccessful experiment of Communism was over for good.

A peaceful revolution in 1989 ushered in a free market and a democratic government. The transformations of the last dozen years are reflected in the countenance of the city. Krakow has evolved over a turbulent thousand years into a very Polish, and at the same time very cosmopolitan town, with a present and a future that promise to be every bit as fascinating and rich as its past.

A HANDFUL OF DATES

965   *Krakow first mentioned in writing, by a Jewish merchant from Cordoba.*

1000   *Construction of the first cathedral on Wawel Hill.*

1241   *The first Tartar raid on Krakow*

1257   *Krakow receives its town charter.*

1364   *King Kazimierz the Great founds a school, later the Krakow University.*

1386   *Grand Duke Władysław Jagiello of Lithuania marries Princess Jadwiga (union between the two countries).*

1536   *The Renaissance Palace on Wawel Hill is completed.*

1609   *King Zygmunt Vasa moves the Polish capital to Warsaw.*

1655-1657   *Swedish occupation of Krakow.*

1772   *First Partition of Poland - Austrians occupy the right bank of the Vistula.*

1793   *Second Partition of Poland - Krakow occupied by the Russians.*

1795   *Third Partition of Poland - Krakow becomes part of Austria.*

1815   *The Krakow Republic proclaimed.*

1846   *Insurrection in Krakow leads to Austrian re-annexation of the city.*

1850   *The Great Fire of Krakow destroys half of the city.*

1867   *Galicia gains autonomy. Gradual modernisation and development of the city.*

1918   *Krakow freed, Austrian troops disarmed*

1939   *Beginning of 5 years' German occupation.*

1941   *Jewish ghetto established by the Nazis in Podgórze.*

1945   *Liberation of Krakow by the Red Army.*

1978   *Cracovian cardinal Karol Wojtyła becomes Pope John Paul II.*

1979   *Krakow is included in the UNESCO World Heritage List.*

1989   *Fall of Communism in Poland.*

2000   *Krakow elected one of the European Cities of Culture.*

Banishing evil, encouraging good: thought for the day on a doorway in ul. Sławkowska.

PART II

GUIDE TO THE CITY

MAJOR SIGHTS

WAWEL HILL

Wawel holds a very special place in Polish history, as the cradle of Polish culture and the spiritual centre of the state. The relics of Bishop Stanislaus (*see p. 9*), patron saint of Krakow and of Poland, are housed here in Wawel Cathedral. The Polish kings ruled from here for centuries, and it is here that they were christened and buried. On important occasions and celebrations, the sound of the royal Zygmunt Bell, cast in 1520, can still be heard from the Cathedral belfry.

Many people believe in the mystical Stone of Wawel Hill, which nobody has ever seen, but whose legend goes back to pre-Christian times. In the Wawel Stone cosmic and earthly energies are believed to converge, and the magic power of this *chakhra* protects the city against evil. *Chakhra* is the Sanskrit word for wheel, a device whose seven energy points around the earth radiate concentrated power.

Winter view of Wawel Castle seen from beyond the Dębnicki Bridge.

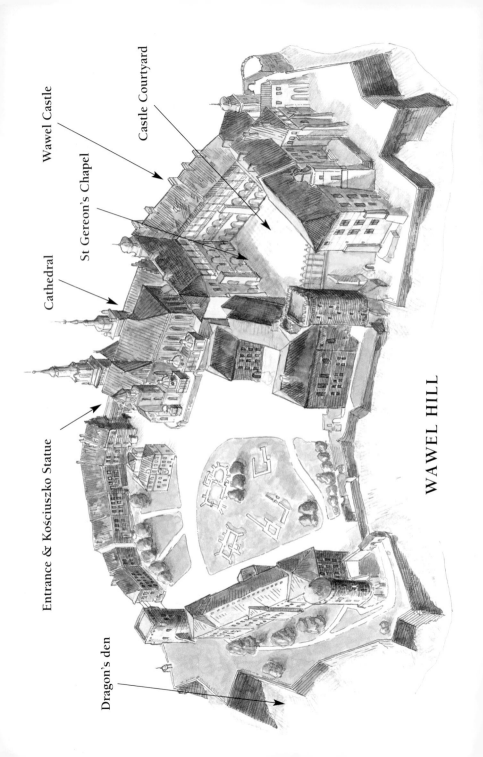

Castle Courtyard

Wawel Castle

St Gereon's Chapel

Cathedral

Entrance & Kościuszko Statue

Dragon's den

WAWEL HILL

Climbing Wawel Hill, you pass through a succession of gates. In the wall on the left, near the first gate, there are bricks engraved with names and dates. These commemorate the sponsors of the castle's restoration, which began after Wawel was returned to the city of Krakow in 1905 (before that it had been used as an Austrian stronghold). On the 16th-century bastion of Władysław IV, there is an equestrian statue of the Polish-American hero Tadeusz Kościuszko (*see p. 48*). Suspended above the entrance to the Cathedral are huge bones - perhaps those of the Wawel Dragon himself, you might think (*see p. 7*). In fact they are fragments of a rhinoceros skull and the jawbones of a cetacean whale and a mammoth. The story goes that should the bones fall loose from the chains that fasten them to the Cathedral wall, history will come to an end. The chains, however, look pretty solid, and so the world seems safe for a while.

WAWEL'S MUSEUMS

Wawel Hill is home to the most important museums in Krakow, and indeed in all Poland. Wawel Castle and the Cathedral are a perfect illustration of the division between Church and State. While the royal apartments and adjoining exhibitions are under the management of the Polish State, the Cathedral is in the care of the Catholic Church. This explains why you have to queue up twice for tickets. "BOTs" (short for "Tourist Services Office" in Polish) sell timed tickets to the Castle and the exhibitions, while entry to the Cathedral (including the Zygmunt Bell Tower and the Royal Crypt) can be obtained from a nun in a small, somewhat hidden ticket office, in a gateway opposite the Cathedral.

THE CATHEDRAL

NB: Numbers in the text refer to numbering on the plan on p. 23.

A cathedral has stood here since around 1000, though the present Gothic building was only begun in 1320, after a series of fires destroyed the previous two. The presbytery was completed about twenty years later and the church was consecrated in 1364. It is a transepted, three-aisled basilica with an ambulatory around the chancel, reminiscent of the Île de France cathedrals. The original Gothic core is discernible, even if rather overshadowed by the cluttered chapels built in the centuries that followed. To the right of the main entrance is the Gothic Chapel of the Holy Cross **1**, its walls adorned with Byzantinesque frescoes, a rare example of mediæval art from Russia. The Ruthenian masters who painted these scenes were brought to Poland when Władysław Jagiello of Lithuania married the young Polish queen Jadwiga in 1386. The chapel contains the tomb of King Kazimierz Jagiello, sculpted by the German master Veit Stoss (*see p. 77*). Like Tutankhamun, Kazimierz is said to have put a curse on the sixteen scholars who exhumed him in 1973. Their deaths were probably the result of a carcinogenic fungus found in the grave. Opposite King Kazimierz's tomb rests his wife, Queen Elżbieta Rakuszanka (Elisabeth Habsburg). All the royal families in Europe to this day are related to this 15th-century couple through the female line.

At the point where the main nave and the transept intercept is the shrine of St Stanislaus **2**. In a fate similar to that of Thomas à Becket, Bishop Stanislaus was murdered and his body hacked to pieces (in 1079). His crime had been to excommunicate King Bolesław the Bold. Legend says that after the burial the martyred Bishop's limbs miraculously reassembled, which was seen as a symbol of Poland's regained unity after the feudal disintegration of the early 12th century. The mausoleum, with

The Renaissance courtyard of Wawel Castle, build by Florentine architects invited to Krakow by King Zygmunt the Old.

GROUND PLAN OF WAWEL
CATHEDRAL

(1) Chapel of the Holy Cross

(2) Shrine of St Stanislaus

(3) Presbytery

(4) Zygmunt Chapel

(5) Tomb of Kazimierz the Great

(6) St Mary's Chapel

(7) Black Crucifix

(8) Zygmunt Tower

(9) Czartoryski Chapel &
entrance to the Royal Crypt

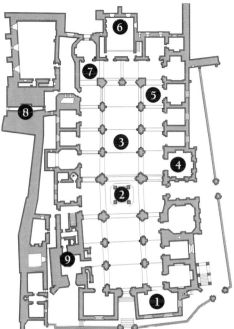

the silver coffin-shrine at its centre, is 17th-century, but the body of this patron saint of Krakow was here by 1254. This place has been regarded as holy, the *Ara Patriae* (altar of the country), ever since. It is to this altar that the Polish Kings brought their spoils of war as an offering: King Władysław Jagiello brought the banners of the Teutonic Knights whom he conquered in the Battle of Grunwald in 1410 (*see p. 93*), and King Jan Sobieski brought Ottoman trophies from the siege of Vienna, from which he emerged triumphant in 1683, effectively putting an end to Ottoman expansion in Europe.

Behind St Stanislaus is the presbytery ❸, with its early Baroque stalls, Flemish tapestries, and 17th-century main altar. Coronation ceremonies took place here. When Queen Jadwiga died, her mortal remains were placed "temporarily" under the main altar - and left there for 450 years. The small coffin containing Jadwiga's bones was moved several times, and a Carrara marble sarcophagus was even created for them in the early 20th century. It was never used, however. In 1987 her remains were placed under the miraculous Black Crucifix in the north side of the ambulatory (*see below*).

The Renaissance Zygmunt Chapel ❹ is a funerary chapel dedicated to Zygmunt the Old and designed by Bartolomeo Berecci of Florence (*see p. 45*). Built between 1519 and 1531, harmonious and exquisitely decorated, it is the most beautiful Renaissance artwork in Poland. The chapel went on to become the mausoleum of all the last Jagiellonians. On the right rest Zygmunt the Old, with his son Zygmunt August, the last male heir of the dynasty, beneath him, and facing the entrance to the chapel, Zygmunt August's sister Queen Anna Jagiellonka. The last two, bearing strong Mannerist features, are the works of Santi Gucci, another Italian architect, who also rebuilt the Cloth Hall on the Rynek (*see p. 36*). The grotesque stuccoes by Giovanni Cini from Siena blend in with the red marble of the effigies and the altar.

Further on on the left is the tomb of Kazimierz the Great ❺, one of the finest monarchs Poland ever had, commissioned in red Hungarian marble by his nephew Ludwik (Lajos) of Hungary, and completed around 1382. The lion under the king's feet symbolises his courage. He is wearing a belt made up of fortified castles – an allusion to his drive to construct and develop the country. During his reign, more new towns were founded and more castles built than ever before. He is most fondly remembered for founding the town of Kazimierz (which bears his name), now a district of Krakow, and for establishing Krakow University.

St. Mary's Chapel ❻ at the east end of the church contains the ornate 16th-century tomb of King Stefan Batory, another work by Santi Gucci. Batory, a Transylvanian prince, owed his throne to his wife, Anna Jagiellonka, the sister of Zygmunt August. His reign was taken up with battles against the might of Ivan the Terrible in Russia, and in wars aimed at forging a Polish-Lithuanian-Swedish alliance to control the Baltic. People say the reason he spent so much time on the battlefield was to escape from his querulous and ill-looking wife, 10 years his senior, and 52 at the time of their marriage.

The Black Crucifix ❼, where Christ addressed Queen Jadwiga from the cross, is to the right of the chapel. Christ is reported to have asked the 12-year-old queen to save the country. This meant marrying the Grand Duke of Lithuania instead of Prince Wilhelm Habsburg, to whom she was pledged as a small child, and who was allegedly much more physically alluring than the wild, pagan Lithuanian. Jadwiga obeyed, and married the Grand Duke, who took the name Władysław Jagiello. Lithuania was converted to Christianity (though in private Władysław in known to have continued to observe pagan

Bishops' tombstones set into the wall on the way up to Wawel Hill.

rites) and annexed to Poland as part of a Union State. Jadwiga was also famed for her many good deeds, including helping the poor and propping up a foundering Krakow University, which was reinstated in 1400 thanks to her endowment. Six hundred years later, Pope John Paul II, proclaimed Jadwiga a saint.

From the northern part of the ambulatory you enter the Zygmunt Tower **8**, which contains the Zygmunt Bell. Commissioned by Zygmunt the Old in 1520, this massive 11-ton copper-and-tin bell is rarely heard, as it only tolls for important state and religious ceremonies. If you reach out and touch the bell's clapper, you are said to be holding its heart, and by doing so all the affairs of your own heart will be resolved. The tower's windows look out on a beautiful view of the city centre.

The Czartoryski Chapel, back down in the church proper, opens onto the Royal Crypts **9**, the resting place of Polish monarchs, heroes and statesmen. The first of the succession of crypts is the spacious and wonderfully simple St Leonard's Crypt, still intact from the original Romanesque cathedral. The kings of Poland are said to gather here every Christmas to discuss the affairs of their country. At the end of their symposium, the sleeping knights of King Bolesław the Brave, who slumber all year amid the rocky peaks of the Tatra mountains, knock on the door of the crypt to enquire whether the country is in need of their help. Despite Poland's various tribulations, King Bolesław has always

The entrance to Wawel Cathedral, with the eagle of the Piast dynasty, to which Kazimierz the Great belonged. It was during his reign that the Cathedral was completed.

responded: "you can go back to sleep, the time has not yet come". The Latin inscription reads: Dormiunt vigilant – the sleepers keep watch.

Wawel Cathedral, with the Royal Crypt and Zygmunt Bell, is open to visitors Mon-Sat 9am-3pm, Sun and religious holidays 12.15 to 3pm. The Cathedral Museum is open Tues-Sun 10am-3pm.

THE CASTLE

To enter the inner courtyard of the castle you go through a gate inscribed *Si Deus nobiscum quis contra nos?* (If God be for us, who can be against us?), and enter a Renaissance courtyard. For a moment you may be under the impression that you are in *quattrocento* Florence - not so surprising, as the Wawel Castle you see today is largely the work of Renaissance architects imported from Italy. The earlier Gothic residence, built by Kazimierz the Great in the 14th century, fell victim to fire in 1499. Soon after the blaze, Prince Zygmunt (later King Zygmunt the Old) hired the Italian architect Francesco Fiorentino. At the beginning of the 16th century work was begun on the western wing, and after Fiorentino's death another Florentine, Bartolomeo Berecci (*see p. 45*), was brought in. He gathered together a team of mostly Italian masons and sculptors, and finally completed the castle in 1536.

The courtyard where we are standing, the very centre of the complex, is an irregular quadrangle. The castle proper consists of three wings to the west, north and east; the southern part is flanked by the curtain wall, while most of the west wing is occupied by the royal kitchens. On closer inspection the

courtyard is not pure Renaissance, but a mixture of local tradition, Gothic influence and Italian characteristics. Whereas the Italian Renaissance adhered to regularity of plan, the Wawel courtyard is large and irregular, though this is partly disguised by the loggias. Another Polish feature is the castle's system of storeys. In Central Europe, unlike in Italy, the ground floor housed utility rooms, the first floor was for private residential quarters, and the second for state ceremonial chambers. These latter had to be much more imposing and therefore double the normal height. The second floor columns are thus twice as long as those on the lower floors, and to create an optical illusion of diminished length, the architect introduced the Gothic device of stone rings set in the column centres. The steep roof, a necessity in snowy Polish winters, was another problem, as a protruding roof overshadowed the decorative capitals. Here the solution was to place stone pitchers on the capitals so that the capitals become mere decorative devices and not keystones. All these tricks lend the courtyard its slim, almost Gothic proportions.

The Renaissance In Krakow is synonymous with the Golden Age of the Jagiello dynasty. A dynamic centre of commerce and crafts at the close of the Middle Ages, Krakow had all the makings a modern manufacturing city. The royal household was the centre of cultural life and artistic patronage, and the Renaissance character of the court was determined by the taste of King Zygmunt the Old. Italian influence in Poland reached its apogee after 1520, when the king married the Milanese princess Bona Sforza. This was reflected not only in the arts but also in customs, language and even cuisine. Queen Bona introduced cabbage, potatoes and tomatoes at court, and they soon became an integral part of traditional Polish fare, part of most people's everyday menu.

Left of the entrance to the courtyard, in the corner, you might see people leaning against the wall, or just standing next to it, taking in what they believe to be its healing energy. Behind that wall are the remains of Saint Gereon's Chapel, where the Wawel Stone is supposed to weave its powerful charm. In the summer of 2001 the wall was fenced off, and a peremptory notice appeared in both Polish and English about how deeply improper it is, in such a historic and holy place, to entertain thoughts about the Wawel Stone, or to "engage in occult practices". The notice was soon taken down, but it made no difference anyway: with or without it, people still believe in the Stone and come to soak up its energies.

INSIDE THE CASTLE

THE ROYAL APARTMENTS: In spite of the Castle's tumultuous history some original features still remain, along with a unique collection of much-travelled 16th-century Arras tapestries. During the Partitions (*see p. 17*) they were taken to Russia, but after the Treaty of Riga in 1921, the Soviet government was obliged to return them. At the beginning of World War II, along with other valuable works of art, they were evacuated to Canada via Romania, France, Malta and England, and did not return until 1961. The tapestries were commissioned by the last of the Jagiellos, King Zygmunt August, from the best Antwerp and Brussels workshops. 136 of the original 356 tapestries survive, including huge Biblical cycles of Paradise, the story of Noah and the building of the Tower of Babel, as well as landscapes and animal scenes depicted with minute attention to detail, with every tiniest leaf and berry picked out in intricate needlepoint.

In the state rooms on the second floor note the coffered ceilings and painted friezes. Murals attributed to Hans Dürer (brother of Albrecht) and Antoni of Wrocław can be found in three rooms south of the Envoy's Staircase (*Schody Poselskie*): the Tournament Room (*Sala Turniejowa*), the Military Review Room (*Sala Przeglądu Wojsk*) and the Audience Hall. The ceiling in the latter is quite unique, and was once adorned with 194 wooden heads sculpted between 1531 and 1535. Only 30 of those heads survive, but even from floor level they are so realistic that you expect them to start chatting away.

"ART OF THE ORIENT" EXHIBITION: The world's largest collection of Turkish tents and banners. Oriental ceramics and weaponry, including the sword of Kara Mustafa, captured by King Jan Sobieski at the siege of Vienna in 1683.

TREASURY: Crowns, sceptres and orbs dating from the Middle Ages to the late 18th century, coronation robes and crosses, and other treasures, including *Szczerbiec*, the coronation sword of the Polish kings.

ARMOURY: A collection of arms and weapons, including the suits of armour of winged Hussars.

The Royal Apartments, "Art of the Orient" exhibition, Treasury and Armoury are open Tues-Sat 9.30am-3pm, Sun 10am-3pm.

If you walk back through the inner and outer courtyards towards the Vistula, you can go down to the river through the Wawel Dragon's Den. The den of this devourer of virgins (*see p. 7*) ironically became a trysting place, as it was conveniently located near the royal court, yet hidden from view. Outside, a splendid statue of the Wawel Dragon, sculpted by artist Bronisław Chromy, spits fire every fifteen minutes to the joyful terror of kids.

RYNEK MARKET SQUARE

The Rynek, 200 metres long by 200 metres wide, is astounding in its dimensions. It is the largest mediæval square in Europe, laid out in 1257 according to the Charter of Krakow.

Throughout the centuries the Market Square was always the scene of major political ceremonies: grand processions of royalty and gentry marched through it on their way to Wawel Castle, and most of Krakow's climactic events took place here. In 1525, Prince Albrecht Hohenzollern of Prussia paid

Interior of the Sukiennice (Cloth Hall), which still functions as a market today.

RYNEK MARKET SQUARE

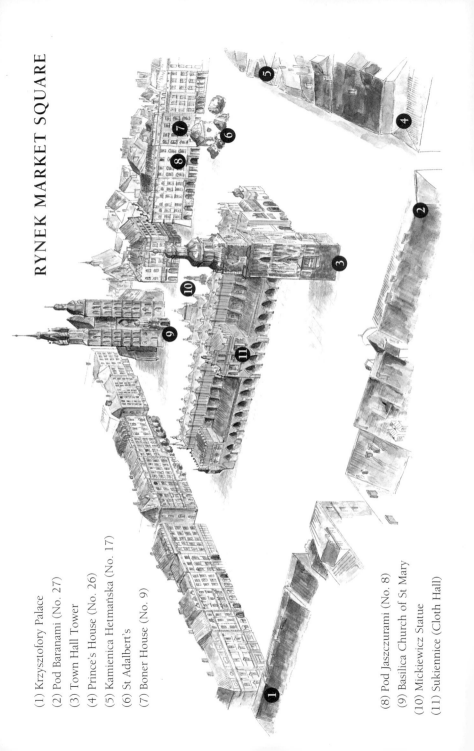

(1) Krzysztofory Palace
(2) Pod Baranami (No. 27)
(3) Town Hall Tower
(4) Prince's House (No. 26)
(5) Kamienica Hetmańska (No. 17)
(6) St Adalbert's
(7) Boner House (No. 9)

(8) Pod Jaszczurami (No. 8)
(9) Basilica Church of St Mary
(10) Mickiewicz Statue
(11) Sukiennice (Cloth Hall)

tribute to the Polish king Zygmunt the Old, while in 1794 national hero Tadeusz Kościuszko swore an oath which marked the beginning of the insurrection against Russia and subsequently Prussia, who had been systematically helping themselves to pieces of Poland (*see p. 13*). In 1918, after a century of Habsburg rule, the Austrian eagles were removed from the Town Hall Tower and the façades around the square, and Krakow became the first Polish town to be free.

There are two ways to circle the square: on foot, or by a horse-drawn cab. The horses and the cabbies, like so many things in Krakow, are, of course, enchanted. The poet Konstanty Ildefons Gałczyński wrote about a magical night journey through the streets and squares of the city in a magical cab, which sadly disappears each morning through the Baroque gate, *amen, in saecula saeculorum.*

The numbers below relate to the numbering on the plan opposite.

1 The Krzysztofory Palace (home to the Historical Museum) in the north corner of the square is steeped in wonderful tales. At night the ghost of the Black Dame patrols the building, and woe betide those who see her, for her appearance spells certain death. In the cellars below the house lives the Krzysztofory devil. He assumes the shape of a rooster, or sometimes a foreign-looking gentleman, and entices girls with promises of instant wealth. Once a cook followed him to the cellar and filled her apron with gold and riches. Although the devil had warned her not to look back, she inevitably took just a peep on leaving, and found her heel caught fast. Luckily she managed to wriggle free and put the money to good use. Another tenant who does not pay the rent at Krzysztofory is the faithful spider servant of Master Twardowski, a 16th-century alchemist who now lives on the moon. Apparently, the spider descends from his lunar dwelling, dangles here to listen to all the latest gossip, and then reports back to his master. Who can blame him? After all, life on the moon must be a bit bereft of titillating scandal. The restaurant at No. 34 is decorated with a frieze retelling the tale of the alchemist and his tale-bearing familiar (Tetmajerowska, *see p. 132*).

So vast are the Krzysztofory cellars that, in addition to all those magical creatures, there's still room enough for a café and art gallery (entrance from Szczepańska), where the 20th-century avant-garde Grupa Krakowska used to meet. Among the members of the group was Tadeusz Kantor (*see p. 38*).

2 The *Pod Baranami* (Palace under the Rams) at No. 27 is so called because sheep used to be sold in the courtyard of what was then an inn. In the cellar, there is the Pod Baranami club, home to the Piwnica Pod Baranami literary cabaret. The troupe's *spiritus movens*, Piotr Skrzynecki, died in 1997. He often used to stroll around the Rynek with a melancholy smile, and a feather stuck in his hat. Now his statue can be seen outside his favourite café, Vis à Vis. The artists of Piwnica continue the tradition of cabaret performances. Always witty and clever, by turns deeply moving and subversively hilarious, Piwnica pod Baranami certainly played a part in shaking the foundations of the "Real Socialist" empire. In search of lyrics, they looked to a nostalgic past and a present which, though oppressive, provided plenty of scope for cutting humour. They sang fragments from Communist manifestoes and contemporary newspaper articles, at once sentimental and subtly ironic.

3 In the south-west corner of the Rynek, the Town Hall Tower – *Wieża Ratuszowa* – is all that remains of the mediæval town hall, demolished at the beginning of 19th century due to its tumbledown state. It was so ruinous that it was deemed a danger to passers-by.

Perhaps Konstanty Ildefons Gałczyński's magical carriage circling the Rynek (see p. 31).

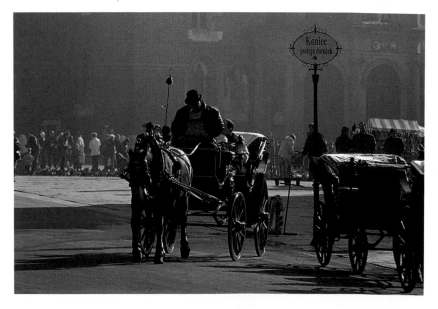

Feeding the Rynek pigeons.

4 No. 26 is the *Kamienica Książęca*, the Princes' House. Turkish envoys stopped here in 1494 on their way to visit the Polish king Jan Olbracht. Their camels and horses caused a local sensation (perhaps the devout populace thought the Magi had come to call). On the corner of the building is the figure of St John Kapistran, a 15th-century monk who preached the Christian crusade against the Ottomans, and another visitor to Krakow who is believed to have stopped here. Now it is home to the British Council (entrance from Wiślna No. 2), with an International Cultural Centre next door at No. 25, occupying the Ravens' House (*Dom pod Kruki*) with The White Raven Café on the ground floor. No. 20, the Potocki Palace, is the now the Goethe Institute.

5 *Kamienica Hetmańska* at No. 17 is one of the oldest houses in Krakow. Enter the bookshop, bear left through the entranceway, and admire its 14th-century vaulting. Next door at *Kamienica Morsztynowska* is the Wierzynek Restaurant. Although it was only established in the 20th century, it claims a mediaeval history. The story runs that in 1364 a wealthy merchant, Mikołaj Wierzynek, gave a feast here in honour of King Kazimierz the Great and his guests at an international congress of monarchs. The guest-list included the Holy Roman Emperor Charles IV, the Hungarian king Lajos the Great, and a host of other kings and princes. Legend says that all the illustrious guests received the golden and silver plates they had been eating off as a parting gift.

6 In the south corner of the Rynek you will see the tiny church of St Adalbert (*see p. 68*), built in the 11th century (before the town charter, in other

words) and remodelled afterwards in the Baroque style. If you go right up to it you will see how the street level of the Market Square has changed since the Middle Ages. The former entrance is over two metres below the present pavement. Just imagine all the ancient Cracovians who have left their footprints underneath the Rynek!

7 No. 9 once belonged to the Boner, then the Firlej family. In 1605 Maryna Mniszchówna married the false Demetrius, usurper of the Tsarist throne, in the family chapel. Funnily enough the groom wasn't present, but sent his secretary Ofnas Własiow to do the thing for him.

8 The *Kamienica pod Jaszczurami* – House under the Lizards – at No. 8 houses a well-known student club, a quiet café by day. The lizards (copies of the originals) above the doorway are perhaps the most exquisite decoration on any of Rynek's tenement houses. The interior boasts the only complete Gothic ribwork of any building on the square. In 1569 the first courier post set off to Venice from the "Italian House" next door at No. 7.

9 The Basilica Church of St. Mary's – *Kościół Mariacki* – towers over the Rynek. Since the early 13th century it has served as the main parish church in

Allegory of Poetry on the Mickiewicz statue, with towers of St Mary's looming in the fog.

*The bugle-call being sounded from
St Mary's tower, complete
with sound-amplification system.*

the city. The present building was built in stages, the main body in the late 14th century, and the adjoining chapels and the spire on the taller tower in the 15th. The taller tower belongs to the municipality, and has an original late Gothic dome topped with a gilded Baroque crown. The towers differ in height, it is said that this is because they were built by two brothers. During construction the jealous architect of the lower and less splendid tower killed his sibling with a knife. Conscience-stricken, he then committed suicide by throwing himself from one of the towers. The murder weapon was hung up in Sukiennice (the Cloth Hall, *see below*) by way of a warning, where a copy of it can still be seen (it is and was a favourite trophy for pranksters).

The higher of the two towers played the role of watchtower. From its windows a bugle call is sounded every hour on the hour. If you listen carefully you will hear that the tune seems to come to a sudden halt. The story goes that when the Tartars were besieging the city in the 13th century, a guardsman climbed the tower to sound the alarm. In mid-blast his throat was pierced by a Tartar arrow, and it is to commemorate this that the tune stops short. In fact the present, popular version of the bugle call is the work of an American, Eric P. Kelly, who came to Krakow as a Kościuszko scholar in 1925, and taught American Studies at the University. Once back in the States he published a book called *The Trumpeter of Cracow* (1928), which won the Newbury Award.

Skirting round the church you come to the charming little pl. Mariacki, once the parish graveyard, which contains the 14th-century church of St Barbara and its adjoining chapel representing the Garden of Gethsemane. In

front of the south door to St Mary's is an old Cracovian stocks, where transgressors were placed on public holidays. The "criminals" thus humiliated included nagging wives, drunken husbands, and young people of both sexes who had flouted the sixth commandment. *For information about the interior of St Mary's, see Religious Monuments on p. 69.*

⑩ The statue of Adam Mickiewicz, the greatest Polish Romantic poet, stands surrounded by Muses and allegorical figures of the Motherland, Science, Courage and Poetry. Mickiewicz is the author of *Pan Tadeusz* (Master Tadeusz), the Polish national epic, which begins with the invocation "Lithuania, my homeland!" This is because when Mickiewicz wrote it Lithuania and Poland were one. Film director Andrzej Wajda has produced a cinematic version of the work, with leading Polish actors reciting sophisticated verse and the usual Wajdaesque wry take on historical events. It took Cracovians a long time to like the monument, but now they hail him as "Adaś!" (a nickname for Adam) as they hurry past to work, school or rendezvous. Flower-sellers dot this section of the Rynek, and have done since the 16th century.

⑪ The Sukiennice – the Cloth Hall – which is and always has been a centre of trade. Built at the beginning of the 13th century, booths were set up here by Kazimierz the Great. After a major fire in the 16th century, the building took on its present Renaissance-Mannerist shape, the work of the Italian architects Santi Gucci and Giovanni Maria Padovano. In the late 19th century the architect Tomasz Pryliński added neo-Gothic arcades and massive central projections in a self-aggrandising, 19th-century railway-station manner, which destroyed the elongated Mannerist lines of the original façades.

Grotesque gargoyles abound on the Sukiennice, some of them designed by Santi Gucci, others added by Pryliński in the 19th century. Pryliński's gargoyles are caricatures of the Krakow City Mayors of the time. The Cloth Hall is now the biggest souvenir market in Krakow. Downstairs it is crowded with stalls selling anything from tacky Wawel dragons to elegant amber jewellery. It is probably the best place in Krakow to get souvenirs.

The upper floor of the Sukiennice is home to an art gallery, part of the National Museum (*see p. 51*). Among the paintings are some historical scenes that took part in this very square: Jan Matejko's *Hołd Pruski* (Prussian Tribute), and *Przysięga Kościuszki* (Kościuszko's Oath) by Michał Stachowicz. One of the most curious paintings is *Szał Uniesień* (Blissful Frenzy) by Władysław Podkowiński. It depicts a naked red-haired lady riding a raging black stallion

into some distant and mysterious nebulae. Gossip-monger Cracovians immediately recognised her as Ewa Kotarbińska, the wife of one of Podkowiński's friends, for whom the painter nurtured an unrequited passion. One day, either outraged at this take on his work, or suffering the pain of rejection, Podkowiński came to the gallery equipped with a ladder and a knife, and started hacking at the canvas. You can still see the marks of his fury, although the painting was later very much restored. Ladders and knives are now banned from every museum in the world - perhaps as a result.

Coming out through the north exit, you face the so-called "A-B" line of the Rynek ("C-D", "E-F" and "G-H" lines also theoretically exist, but somehow the names never caught on). Walking along it you will glimpse some lovely emblems: the white eagle at No. 45, the severed head of St John the Baptist at No. 44, and the sun at No. 43. In the summer the pavements fill with little gardens, *ogródki* - outdoor cafés, in other words - and this A-B line offers the best view of the whole, as well as enjoying the sun for the longest time.

TADEUSZ KANTOR
1915-1990

Creator of drama and images, this master attended the Krakow Academy of Fine Art, and lived and died in the city. His extraordinary creations, which were at once absurd, ground-breaking and spectacular, had a profound influence on international theatre, and Kantor has gone down as the Polish magister of the performing arts. Works like *The Dead Class*, *Today is my Birthday* and *Wielopole-Wielopole*, with their bizarre take on power and absence, liberated western theatrical practices and provided a new way of interpreting "all the world's a stage". Kantor's Cricot-2 Theatre showed that theatre can be produced out of rags, handmade wooden props and old handbags - that the idea and energy behind the performance is more vital than lush sets and costumes, and that creative energies are put to the test when instilling life into an old broom handle or a set of broken beads. Kantor also painted and made collages and installations, which manifest the raw drive of his theatre pieces. You can visit the Cricoteka (at ul. Kanonicza No. 5 in the centre of town, *see Map References on p. 156*), which houses the Cricot-2 archives and where they have video tapes of Kantor's works as well as a collection of his writings and drawings.

ARCHITECTURE

As with any European city fortunate enough to be allowed to develop gradually and almost organically without major catastrophes, Krakow is like an open book of architectural history. A succession of styles blends into a palimpsest of Romanesque, Gothic, Renaissance, Baroque, Classicist, and Art Nouveau. Later departures towards Socialist Realism stand outside the Old Town walls, and although architecturally the city shows little inclination to rush headlong into the future, there are interesting examples of contemporary architecture as well.

Female personification of Industry from Mączyński's Chamber of Commerce.

A CHRONOLOGY
OF KRAKOW ARCHITECTURE WITH
SURVIVING EXAMPLES

The top of St Adalbert's Church with the
towers of St Mary's behind it.

ROMANESQUE &
GOTHIC

In the 11th century, Krakow's ascent
to power as the seat of the court stim-
ulated construction. Romanesque
Krakow remains almost intact within
St. Leonard's crypt at Wawel, and
also, despite later additions and alter-
ations, in the churches of St Adalbert
(*see p. 68*) and St Andrew (*see p. 87*).

The Gothic period added more
solid foundations to the city.
Although the Gothic layer is often
partly hidden beneath later accre-
tions, it is clearly discernible in the
windows and houses of ul.
Kanonicza, in vaulted cellars, and in
perpendicular church naves. Among
the most beautiful incarnations of
the Gothic in Krakow are the
churches of St Mary (*see p. 34 and p.
68*) and St Katherine (*see p. 70*), the
Dominican and Franciscan churches
(*see p. 69*), as well as the Collegium
Maius and Collegium Iuridicum
belonging to the Jagiellonian
University.

THE RENAISSANCE
PERIOD

The Golden Age of Krakow is syn-
onymous with the Renaissance and
Mannerist period in its architecture.
Renaissance architecture came to
Krakow direct from Florence, when
Italian architects were invited by
King Zygmunt to rebuild the Royal
Castle. These architects included
Francis of Florence (Francesco
Fiorentino), Bartolomeo Berecci (*see
p. 45*), Giovanni Maria Mosca (called

Padovano), Santi Gucci - and a single Pole: Jan Michałowicz from Urzędów. The best examples of Renaissance architecture in Krakow can be found on Wawel Hill (*see p. 26*), in the Castle's inner courtyard, and in the Zygmunt Chapel, dubbed the pearl of the Central European Renaissance, and used as a model for countless later renditions. Renaissance architectural elements can also be found in the houses of ul. Kanonicza, and in Rynek's Sukiennice (Cloth Hall). Although plenty of Renaissance synagogues were constructed in Kazimierz, including Kupa and Poppera as well as the splendid Isaac's Synagogue (*see p. 73*), there is not a single Renaissance church. This is because the Gothic building movement was so strong and solid that it had provided the city with its full complement of churches for the next two centuries and more.

THE BAROQUE ERA

Churches come to the fore again in this period, the age of the Jesuits and the Counter Reformation. So many were built in Krakow, in fact, that they earned the city the nickname "Little Rome". Compelling in their lavish glory, histrionic in their *trompe l'oeil* and tricks of shadow and light, Baroque churches were clustered with sculpted skulls and bones, evoking *memento mori* and *vanitas vanitatum* against the froth of the gilded angels. Among the multitude of Baroque churches in Krakow, the most beautiful are the University Church of St Anne, (*see p. 75*) designed by a Dutchman, Tylman of Gameren; the Piarist Church (*see p. 83*) by Kasper Bażanka (*see below*) and Francesco Placidi. The *tour de force*, however, is the Jesuit church of SS. Peter & Paul (*see p. 72*), the first Baroque church in Krakow, modelled on the Il Gesù Jesuit church in Rome.

NEO-CLASSICISM & HISTORICISM

From the end of the 18th century until World War I, Krakow was a provincial city in the great Austro-Hungarian Empire. Many traces of the Habsburg presence in Krakow can still be seen today. In 1784, Emperor Joseph II founded the new, Classicist town of Podgórze, now a district of Krakow, perfectly symmetrical with its trapezoid main square.

In the 19th century, Classicism and Historicism were the dominant styles. It was during this period that tenets concerning the relationship between function and architectural style were laid down, and these tenets prevailed right the way across the Austro-Hungarian empire. For an academic building, neo-Renaissance was considered the most appropriate style, for a church neo-Gothic or neo-Romanesque, and for a theatre neo-Baroque. Cracovian examples of this include the Słowackiego Theatre (see p. 92), and the neo-Renaissance Academy of Fine Art, built along the Planty Ring as one of the grand, imposing new buildings constructed along it when the old city walls were demolished. The Tempel Synagogue in Kazimierz is another interesting example of "neo" Historicist styles. This was also the era of the *enfant terrible* of Krakow architecture, Teodor Talowski (see p. 47). His buildings, including the House under the Spider (in Karmelicka) and the House under the Singing Frog (at the corner of Retoryka and Piłsudskiego), stand at the crossroads between Historicism and Art Nouveau, with a distinct, precocious post-modern twist, well before postmodernism had been invented.

ART NOUVEAU

To create a synthesis of all the arts is a postulate of *Gesamtkunstwerk*, central to the Art Nouveau movement.

Krakow's examples include Czynciel's House at the corner of Rynek Główny and Mariacki, the Palace of Art (see p. 46), the former Chamber of Commerce and Industry, and the Jesuit Church in ul. Kopernika, by Franciszek Mączyński (see p. 46). The local Art Nouveau style, however, found its fullest expressions in interiors, such as the Jama Michalika (Floriańska 45, see p. 91 & p. 136) or the Medical Society building (Radziwiłłowska 4). The turn of the 19th and 20th centuries was a time of great renovation projects, which often provided the opportunity for a striking juxtaposition of styles, as in the Franciscan church, adorned with magnificent murals and stained-glass windows by Stanisław Wyspiański (see p. 53). Another interesting Krakow building of the period is the School of Industry (Al. Mickiewicza 5), with its strong vernacular features and folk motifs.

THE INTER-WAR PERIOD

Some of the most interesting and typical examples of architecture between the two world wars include the Press Palace (former department store) at the corner of Starowiślna and Wielopole, designed by Stryjeński

and Mączyński (*see p. 46*), the new building of the National Museum (*see p. 52*), and the Jagiellonian Library. These last two, both on Al. Mickiewicza, exemplify the prevailing monumental, classicising functionalism of Cracovian architecture at the time.

THE SECOND WORLD WAR

During the Nazi occupation and war, Krakow's green common of Błonia narrowly escaped being converted into a Nazi residential district, plans and designs for which were ready in 1941. Instead, the Germans built their *Nur für Deutsche* residential blocks, typical *Licht und Luft* Third-Reich architecture, along Reichstrasse (now Królewska). Ironically, the residential blocks on Lea and Chopina were designed by Jewish architects who had to flee when Hitler came to power. Today Nazi architectural intervention remains, of all places, on Wawel Hill, in the block that closes off the inner courtyard of the castle.

SOCIALIST REALISM

In 1949 Krakow received the unwelcome gift of a steel industry and model socialist town to go with it: Nowa Huta (main architect: Tadeusz

Interior of the Słowackiego Theatre, a typical example of Cracovian Historicism.

Jesuit Church of SS. Peter and Paul, the first Baroque building in the city.

Ptaszycki). It is a bold geometric plan of regular blocks radiating from a central square, which adheres to principles of Renaissance and Classicist town planning. The building that houses the steelworks administration is known as the "Doge's Palace", and is a marriage of Socialist Realism with neo-Renaissance. The clarity of the original centre of Nowa Huta blurs and becomes less distinct in its suburbs (*see p. 121*).

CONTEMPORARY

Today the city is fairly conservative and still awaits a glass pyramid to its Louvre. Here and there, however, some interesting examples of contemporary architecture can be found: Romuald Loegler's (b. 1940) University of Economics at Rakowicka 27, and the new annexe to the Jagiellonian Library at Al. Mickiewicza 22, which, although modern, still manages to respect the lines of the older building to which it is joined. There are also the Cracovia Hotel (a true sign of its times; *see p. 142*) and the Kijów Cinema at Al. Krasińskiego 34, both by Witold Cęckiewicz (*see p. 47*). Perhaps the most interesting modern building in Krakow, however, is the Manggha

Centre of Japanese Art and Technology (*see p. 52*), the work of the eminent Japanese architect Arata Isozaki. Manggha's gentle wave (or leaf) shape is soothing in itself, and also its site, across river from the historic Wawel Hill, gives the mass a weightlessness which contrasts with the accumulation of historical styles that stand facing it.

A HANDFUL OF ARCHITECTS AND THEIR BUILDINGS

BARTOLOMEO BERECCI (c.1480-1537) - Florentine architect largely responsible for transforming Wawel Castle from a Gothic stronghold into a sophisticated Renaissance palace. Completed in 1536, the result has been described as the best example of Florentine Renaissance architecture outside Florence. King Zygmunt the Old also commissioned his funerary chapel (*see p. 24*) from Berecci, and this started a fashion in Poland for chapels with domes, as well as inspiring a host of copies of the Zygmunt Chapel itself. There are over a hundred imitations of it throughout Poland. Berecci settled in Krakow, married twice, each time to a local woman, and became citizen of Kazimierz, where he was a councillor from 1533. He was mysteriously murdered in the Rynek, in front of house No. 28, in 1537, some say at the hands of a fellow Italian architect jealous of his success (the house in fact belonged to the archi-tect Santi Gucci at the time), some say as part of a family vendetta. Nine years later, his son Sebastian also met a mysterious end... Berecci is buried in the Corpus Christi church in Kazimierz.

KASPER BAŻANKA (after 1680-1726) - Trained in Rome under the Jesuit father and master of the *trompe l'oeil* Andrea Pozzo. He settled in Krakow in around 1710, where he worked mainly on church commissions, putting his mastery of illusionist perspectives and understanding of how to play with light to full use. The top of the Wawel Cathedral clock tower is his, as is the enclosure outside the church of SS. Peter and Paul (*see p. 85*), the church where he is buried.

TADEUSZ STRYJEŃSKI (1849-1943) - Studied at the École des Beaux Arts in Paris and in Zurich under Gottfried Semper, architect of London's Albert Hall. Between 1874

Angel above the entrance to Mączyński's church on ul. Kopernika.

and 1877 he worked as state architect in Lima, Peru, but "too many revolutions and unstable conditions" induced him to return to Europe. On settling in Krakow, under Austrian rule at the time, he had to obtain Austrian citizenship in order to be allowed an architect's licence. This caused him considerable difficulty, as the imperial police had decided that he was a nihilist and a socialist agent. His works in Krakow include the District Savings Society (Pijarska 1), his own villa, "Pod Stańczykiem" at Batorego 12, and the redevelopment of the Stary Teatr with Mączyński (*see below*). The former neo-Renaissance theatre building was entirely transformed by the architects in 1903-6. A floral frieze on the façades connects the building's two asymmetric parts, and above the entrance soars a light steel ornamental roof, which must have seemed very daring at the time.

FRANCISZEK MĄCZYŃSKI (1874-1947) - Studied in Vienna and Paris as well as in Krakow. The first architect to introduce Art Nouveau to Polish buildings, and the most prolific architect of his day in Krakow. He set up a studio together with Stryjeński, and worked on the rede-

velopment of the Stary Teatr (corner of Jagiellońska and pl. Szczepański). His style gradually evolved from Art Nouveau through Modernism to Functionalism. One of Mączyński and Stryjeński's joint projects was the Press Palace on Wielopole. Mączyński's other buildings include the Palace of Art (on pl. Szczepański), the best example of a *Gesamtkunstwerk* in Krakow, synthesising different artistic disciplines (*see p. 94*), as well as the former Chamber of Commerce and Industry, also known as the House under the Globe (on the corner of Basztowa and Długa). This building incorporates neo-Gothic features as well as more contemporary influences, but is relatively ascetic and does not revel in an excess of ornament. The ship sailing on the façade symbolises trade, a dialogue with the viewer that is typical of the architecture of the period, which was dubbed *architecture parlante* (talking architecture).

TEODOR TALOWSKI (1857-1910) - Eccentric and idiosyncratic architect of whimsical-looking apartment blocks, uniting elements of the Gothic with the Romantic in a style sometimes described as "painterly Historicism". The mystery-loving Talowski crams in architectural ref-erences, borrowed Latin aphorisms and subtle jokes, and adorns his trademark, raw brick asymmetrical façades with grotesque creatures, vines and other greenery. He also liked to invest his buildings with invented histories. The House under the Spider at Karmelicka 35, for example, bears the marks of a siege that never took place. Other works by Talowski include the House under the Donkey at Retoryka 9, the House under the Singing Frog at Retoryka 1 and Festina Lente at Retoryka 7.

WITOLD CĘCKIEWICZ (b. 1924) - Perhaps the best-known contemporary architect in Krakow. His works from the 1960s, which include the Cracovia Hotel and the Kijów Cinema on Al. Krasińskiego, show some influence by Le Corbusier, though the Cracovia Hotel also confirms the clichés of 1960s soulless-ness. Cęckiewicz planned a mosaic for the rear façade of the cinema, but building materials were scarce in the lean days of Communism, and only three kinds of tile were available. Undaunted, Cęckiewicz pitched in to help manufacture the tiles himself. In 1978 he won the Indian govern-ment's Building of the Year prize for his Polish Embassy in New Delhi.

A HANDFUL OF HEROES

Some of the famous figures from Krakow and Polish history, after whom streets are named, and who occur and recur in this book.

KAZIMIERZ THE GREAT (1310-1370)
The last of the Piast dynasty, famous for strengthening and developing the country. He established new towns including Kazimierz and Kleparz, and founded the Krakow Academy (later the Jagiellonian University) in 1364.

JADWIGA OF ANJOU, (c.1374-1399)
Niece of Kazimierz the Great and daughter of the King of Hungary, Jadwiga was married, at the age of 12, to the Lithuanian Grand Duke Władysław Jagiello. The marriage achieved the union of the two states and made Poland the largest kingdom in Europe. Benefactress of the Krakow Academy, which was restored thanks to her bequest. She was recently canonised by the Catholic Church.

ZYGMUNT THE OLD (1467-1548)
Ruled at Krakow at the time of its Golden Age. A great promoter of the arts, married to the Milanese princess Bona Sforza, he rebuilt the Royal Castle in the Renaissance style.

TADEUSZ KOŚCIUSZKO (1746-1817)
General and military engineer who fought in the American War of Independence (at the sieges of Saratoga and West Point). Returned to Poland to lead the doomed 1794 National Uprising, aimed at preventing Russia, Prussia and Austria from partitioning the country. When the Uprising failed, he was imprisoned at St Petersburg, and then spent the rest of his life in exile. He died in Switzerland.

JÓZEF PIŁSUDSKI (1867-1935)
The key prophet and architect of Poland's bid for independence after World War I. He became the head of the independent Polish state, the Second Republic, on 11th November 1918. Buried in the Wawel Crypt.

KAROL WOJTYŁA (b. 1920)
One of Krakow's youngest-ever bishops and then cardinals, an actor in the Rhapsodic Theatre, poet, playwright and passionate mountaineer. In 1978, he became Pope John Paul II. He has visited Krakow several times since, where his masses always draw crowds of thousands.

ART & MUSEUMS

There are an estimated 2.3 million works of art in Krakow, and most of them have found their way into the city's numerous museums. Wawel Castle, the Czartoryski Collection, or the Jagiellonian University Museum offer much to marvel at, including mediæval arrases, Renaissance masterpieces and the astrolabes that Copernicus pondered over. The best of Krakow's museums, both for permanent and temporary exhibitions, are given below.

NB: The museums of Wawel Hill are dealt with in the Major Sights section on p. 19.

Sign outside one of Krakow's many and various art galleries.

THE NATIONAL MUSEUM OF KRAKOW

This museum is divided into several sections spread across the city. The best are given ˡ ˑ ˡ ˑ

CZARTORYSKI MUSEUM: Lady Izabela Czartoryska (1746-1835) started collecting memorabilia of the past, in the sentimental fashion of her time. By the beginning of the 19th century the collection had grown so much that a "Sibyl's Temple" and a "Little Gothic House" had to be built at the Czartoryski residence in Puławy, to hold the assorted treasures. After the fall of the anti-Russian November Uprising (1830), in which the Czartoryski family were implicated, part of the collection was secretly removed to Paris, where it continued to grow. About forty years later, prince Władysław Czartoryski decided to bring his family treasures back to Poland, and he chose Krakow to house his collection. The municipality provided the former arsenal, the prince bought adjacent buildings, and the whole was revamped in neo-Gothic style.

The museum was opened in 1876, and even in the 21st century it has lost nothing of its 19th-century charm, cosiness and sentimental aura. In true 19th-century style art is mixed with history: personal objects

belonging to Polish kings and heroes sit next to a wonderful collection of European painting. You will find Rembrandt's *Landscape with the Good Samaritan* also known as *Landscape before the Storm*, and Leonardo da Vinci's beautiful *Lady with an Ermine*. The lady who tamed the wild ermine is probably Cecilia Gallerani, a mistress of Lodovico Sforza, Prince of Milan. The ermine is thought to be an allusion to their romance. Lodovico Sforza was nicknamed Ermellino and the Greek word for the creature is Gale, which is part of the lady's name.
Sw. Jana 19. Open Tues & Thurs 9am-

3.30pm, Weds & Fri 11am-6pm, Sat & Sun 10am-3.30pm. Closed Mon and every third Sun.

SUKIENNICE PAINTING GALLERY: The showcase for Polish history painting. Here you will find huge and imposing historical scenes by Jan Matejko (*see p. 54*). Look for Piotr Michałowski, the greatest Polish Romantic painter, as well as Władysław Podkowiński and Józef Chełmoński.
Rynek Główny 1-3. Open Tues, Thur 9am-3.30pm, Weds, Fri 11am-6pm, Sat and Sun 10am-3.30pm. Closed Mon and every third Sun.

Red brick interior of the Manggha Centre of Japanese Art and Technology, which stands across the river from Wawel Hill.

MANGGHA CENTRE OF JAPANESE ART AND TECHNOLOGY: A magnificent collection of woodblock prints, pottery, Samurai armour and more, assembled by the Oriental enthusiast Feliks "Manggha" Jasieński (*see p. 137*) at the turn of the 20th century. Manggha was a nickname bestowed on him because of his passion for the Orient. The collection had to wait almost a hundred years for a proper, permanent exhibition space. It owes its existence to the patronage of Oscar-winning film director Andrzej Wajda and the generosity of many Japanese people. Designed by the Japanese architect Arata Isozaki, the building is interesting in itself. Its terrace opens onto the river and Wawel castle opposite. Manggha also has a concert hall, a Japanese cafeteria and tea room, plus a museum shop.

Al. Konopnickiej 26. Open Tues-Sun 10am-6pm, closed every third Sun.

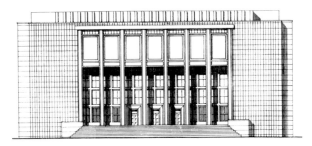

NATIONAL GALLERY - MAIN BUILDING: Designed in 1934 by the architects Boleslaw Schmidt, Janusz Juraszynski and Juliusz Dumnicki. The first stage of construction was completed by 1939; but the final outcome is a scaled-down version of the original plan. Although very monumental, and not free from the authoritarian flavour of 1930s architecture, it makes an interesting modern museum. The permanent collection includes displays of Polish military paraphernalia, and an applied arts collection, with complete interiors from different historical periods. Notable for its many good temporary exhibitions, too, though the Polish 20th-century collection is currently closed for restoration.

Al. 3 Maja 1 (opposite Błonia and the Cracovia Hotel). Open Tues & Thurs 9am-3.30 pm, Weds & Fri 11am-6 pm, Sat & Sun 10am-3.30pm. Closed Mon and every third Sun.

TWO MAJOR KRAKOW ARTISTS
AND THEIR MUSEUMS

STANISŁAW WYSPIAŃSKI (1869-1907)

"Krakow is a city of dreams and phantoms", wrote this great painter, poet and playwright, born in Krakow in 1869. Except for a few years of study in Paris, he spent his whole life here, and his art draws from the city's past and transforms its present. For Wyspiański, Art Nouveau revealed the relatedness of the arts, their interpretation, a movement towards synthesis. In his work we recognise the late 19th-century desire to create a *Gesamtkunstwerk*. Wyspiański's art was universal. He was a playwright and director, set and costume designer, a poet and painter, maker of stained glass windows, murals and furniture and an interior designer. His work fuses modernity and tradition, Polish folk art and Western heritage, Greek culture, Slavic mythology and Christianity, and is resonant with symbols and allegories. His great love for the city made him draw it and paint it constantly. He also worked on several restoration projects, some of which became masterpieces in themselves. This is the case with the brilliant frescoes and stained glass windows of the Franciscan Church (*see p. 69*).

Wyspański's Art Nouveau masterpiece "God the Father" in the Franciscan Church.

The Wyspiański Museum is a biographical collection of the artist's life and work, and includes designs for stained-glass windows, lovely pastel portraits of sleeping children, original turn-of-the-century furniture made to his design, drawings of theatrical costumes, and his plan for the metamorphosis of Wawel Hill. In 1904, when Wawel was regained from the Austrians, Wyspiański had the visionary idea of turning it into a

"Polish Acropolis", a political and cultural centre complete with a mock Roman forum and amphitheatre. A mind-boggling concept - it never came to fruition - but a model of the Wawel Acropolis can be seen in the museum.

Kanonicza 9. Open Tues, Thurs 11am-6pm, Weds, Fri 9am-3.30pm, Sat, Sun 10am-3.30pm. Closed Mon and every third Sun.

JAN MATEJKO (1838-1893) - A major painter of historical and battle scenes, Matejko trained in Munich and Vienna. His enormous canvases are brim-full of theatricality and emotion, which often takes some-thing of a nationalist turn. Krakow was part of the Austrian empire for all of Matejko's creative life, which perhaps explains why so much of his work harks back to Krakow's past military glories. One of his crowning achievements are the murals in St Mary's Basilica on the Rynek (*see p. 71*). The museum dedicated to Matejko is housed in the building where he lived. Apart from his paint-ings there are also various objects he collected and used as props for his works.

Floriańska 41. Open Tues, Thur 9am-3.30pm, Weds, Fri 11am-6pm, Sat, Sun 10am-3.30pm. Closed Mon and every third Sun.

Interior of a peasant home in the Ethnographic Museum.

OTHER MUSEUMS

CRICOTEKA

Centre documenting the work of theatre maestro Tadeusz Kantor with the Cricot-2 Theatre. Videos of performances, as well as drawings and jottings by Kantor are on display. Every year at noon on 8th December, the anniversary of Kantor's death, a living tableau of characters from his plays is performed by the faithful Cricot-2 actors.
Kanonicza 5. Open Mon-Fri 8am-4pm

ARCHAEOLOGICAL MUSEUM

Located in the former prison of St Michael. Exhibits include Egyptian mummies and the totem-shaped statue of Światowid, a pre-Christian god of the Slavonic tribes. Światowid has four faces, symbolising the four corners of the world.
Poselska 3. Open Mon-Wed 9am-2pm; Thurs 2pm-6pm; Fri, Sun 10am-2pm. Closed Sat.

ARCHIDIOCESAL MUSEUM

Religious art and ecclesiastical treasures. Among the museum's exhibits is the oldest surviving Polish painting (second half of the 13th century), a tempera on wood of St Agnes and St Katherine. It also houses the room in which Karol Wojtyła lived for 16 years before he became Pope.
Kanonicza 19. Open Mon-Fri 10am-4pm; Sat, Sun 10am-3pm.

ETHNOGRAPHIC MUSEUM

In the former town hall of Kazimierz, this museum shows Polish folk culture and art, particularly from the Krakow region.
Pl. Wolnica 1. Open Mon 10am-6pm; Wed-Fri 10am-3pm; Sat, Sun 10am-2pm.

PHARMACY MUSEUM
OF THE COLLEGIUM MEDICUM, JAGIELLONIAN UNIVERSITY

One of three such museums in Europe, tracing the history of the pharmacist's profession, through interiors of old pharmacies, mortars and majolica utensils, and plenty of curious appliances. There is also a reconstructed alchemist's room.
Floriańska 25. Tues 3pm-7pm; Wed-Sun 11am-2pm. Closed first and fifth Sat of the month.

Finely detailed mid 19th-century pistol in the Krakow Historical Museum.

JAGIELLONIAN UNIVERSITY MUSEUM

A curious collection of memorabilia from the oldest University in Poland. The most valuable exhibits include an early 16th-century Jagiellonian Globe showing the newly-discovered America, a Moorish astrolabe made in 1054 in Cordoba, and a collection of 15th-century astronomical and astrological instruments belonging to Copernicus (*see p. 88*).

Ticket Office by a narrow staircase in the first floor loggia of the Collegium Maius courtyard.

Collegium Maius, Jagiellońska 15.

Open Mon-Fri 11am-2.20pm (last tickets) and Sat 11am-1.20pm. For an English language tour, call (48-12) 422-05-49 or 422-10-33 ext. 1307, Fax: (48-12) 422-27-34.

KRAKOW HISTORICAL MUSEUM

A permanent exhibition of the history and art of Krakow. At Christmas, it is host to an exhibition of *szopki krakowskie* - nativity scenes made in Krakow, a centuries old tradition.

Rynek Główny 35. Open every second Tues, Wed, Fri, Sat, Sun 9am-3.30pm, Thur 11am-6pm. Closed Mon, every

alternate Tues, and the second Sat and Sun of the month.

MUSEUM OF MUNICIPAL ENGINEERING

The only such museum in the world, situated in an old tram terminus built around 1900, this museum deals with the history of technology and developments in municipal engineering. Permanent exhibitions include a history of Krakow's trams, and an account of the renowned A. Rothe candle factory.

Św. Wawrzyńca 15. Open Tue-Sun 10am-4pm (1 October–30 April until 2pm).

TEMPORARY EXHIBITION VENUES

PALACE OF ART (PAŁAC SZTUKI): Gallery of the Fine Arts Society which hosts temporary exhibitions. Quality is variable, but the building itself is interesting (*see p. 95*).

Pl. Szczepański 4. Open Tues-Sun 11am-6pm.

BUNKER OF ART (BUNKIER SZTUKI): The term "Bunker" began as a derisory nickname, but a few years ago it actually became official, and has now gained its place on the city map. With its clean lines and the clever incorporation of a mediæval tenement house into its structure, this is in fact rather a good building. Nowadays the Bunker of Art offers a well-paced succession of contemporary art shows, exhibitions and accompanying events. It's almost always worth popping in for a look.

Pl. Szczepański 3a (entrance from the Planty). Open Tues-Sun 11am-6pm.

KRAKOW & FILM

ANDRZEJ WAJDA (b. 1926)
Wajda graduated from the Krakow Academy of Fine Art. Much of his creative energy was taken from the city, and he has given back plenty more, including the wonderful gift of Manggha, the Japanese Museum (*see p. 52*). He is probably Poland's best-known film and theatre director, winner of the César (1982), Felix (1990) and Oscar (2000) awards. His films include *Man of Marble* and *Man of Iron*, the first telling the story of the building of Communism, along with the Nowa Huta steelworks (*see p. 121*), and the other the story of Solidarity and Poland's struggle for independence. At the Stary Teatr (*see p. 96*) he directed famous productions of perhaps the greatest Polish play of all time, *Wesele*, by Wyspiański (*see p. 53*), as well as of Shakespeare's Hamlet.

FILM FACTS

Of all Polish cities, Krakow – both indoors and outdoors – is the favourite cinematic location. The Rynek appears in Krzysztof Kieślowski's *Double Life of Veronica*, and Kazimierz in Steven Spielberg's *Schindler's List*. The latter even gave rise to *Schindler's List* theme tours.

Billy Wilder was born on 1st June 1906 in nearby Sucha, and it was in Krakow where he saw his first movies. Years later, in Hollywood, he made *Sunset Boulevard* and *Some Like It Hot*.

The year 1946 saw the stage debut of the 12-year-old Roman Polański. He played the main character in *The Fate of a Drummer-Boy* in a children's theatre.

Krakow has many movie theatres, including the historic Sztuka (Św. Jana 6) and Wanda (Św. Gertrudy 5). Foreign films are always shown in the original version, subtitled in Polish.

Cracovian Film Festivals include the Krakow International Short Film Festival in May, Krak-Cult-Film in June, the Animated Films Workshop in November, and the superb Silent Movie Festival in December, when rockers, jazzmen, and philharmonic orchestras perform live to black-and-white genre classics.

MUSIC & FESTIVALS

A bird's-eye view of the mediæval Old Town of Krakow reveals the contours of a lute. Some people say this is a sign that Krakow was bound to possess a high degree of musical sensibility. Each and every hour of Cracovian time is celebrated by trumpet voluntaries launched to the four corners of the earth from St Mary's Basilica in the Rynek (*see p. 35*). The deep, D-sharp note of the Zygmunt Bell is rarely rung from Wawel Cathedral, and yet Cracovians believe that its sound, which carries out to a radius of 50 kilometres, has the power to scatter rain clouds and bring sunny weather (and Cracovians are not famed for their credulity).

Ancient and contemporary, religious and secular - music of all kinds resounds in Krakow's Philharmonic Hall, in the naves of the city's churches and in museums-turned-concert halls. In the summer, when music tumbles out into the courtyards, squares, and streets of the city, Krakow's feathered

Cracovian folk band in full regalia.

The Sinfonietta Cracovia rehearsing at the Philharmonic Hall.

population joins these outdoor concerts, and the birdsong, along with the man-made melodies, mingles and carries far out into the ozone. Don't be too surprised if you also hear the cacophonous sound of jubilant young boys, just released from their military service, rushing around the streets in garishly colourful shawls of their own making, singing their lungs out in tuneless ecstasy.

Venues mentioned in this section and/or streets where they are located can be found in the Map References on p. 156.

RELIGIOUS MUSIC

Krakow's musical history goes back to the 11th century, when Benedictine monks taught Gregorian chant at Wawel. The soul-stirring plainsong of that age can still be heard at sung mass in the Dominican Church on Dominikańska. Music has had many ready ears and worthy protectors in this city. King Władysław Jagiello literally fell victim to his love of music. He loved the song of the nightingale so much

that he went out to listen to it in the chill morning and caught a cold. In 1393, during the reign of Jagiello and his wife Jadwiga, the first psalter choir and ensemble was established. A hundred years later, Cracovian composers Mikołaj Gomółka and Cyprian Bazylik were fêted around Europe. In 1543, King Zygmunt the Old founded a singers' consort, which sang prayers in the Zygmunt Chapel at Wawel Castle each day before dawn. This tradition continued until 1872, and was rekindled in 1983 by the Capella Cracoviensis. The Festival of Early Music in the autumn echoes those early Cracovian musical traditions.

CLASSICAL MUSIC & MUSIC VENUES

Krakow abounds with classical music festivals. Among the most famous are the Easter Beethoven Festival, which usually starts a week before Easter and culminates on Easter Monday, and "Music in Old Krakow", usually held in the second half of August. Check out the programme at the Philharmonic Hall (*Zwierzyniecka 1, Tel: 429-13-45; box office open Tues-Thur 2pm-7pm, Fri till 7.30pm; Sat-Sun an hour before the concert*), not just for the local orchestra, but for various guest performers coming in from all over the world. One famous visiting musician, Nigel Kennedy, so fell in love with Krakow that he bought a flat in Floriańska, and became a seasonal resident. Apart from the obvious venue of the Philharmonic Hall, concerts are also performed in Wawel Castle, in the Ceremonial Hall of the Jagiellonian University, and in a host of city churches: St Mary's, SS. Peter and Paul and the Franciscan Church, to name only a few. The Florianka concert hall at the Music Academy (Basztowa 8), the Manggha Centre (Al. Konopnickiej 26), as well as the Jewish Cultural Center in Kazimierz (Meiselsa 17) complete the list of indoor venues, but Krakow's courtyards and squares willingly become musical stages in the summer.

The city of Krakow has several orchestras, including the Philharmonic Orchestra, the Capella Cracoviensis, and, best of them all, the Sinfonietta Cracovia, directed by Robert Kabara, while John Neal Axelrod, who flies in from New York, is a frequent guest conductor.

KLEZMER

In addition to philharmonic classics, Nigel Kennedy has also played his violin with the Krakovian klezmer band Kroke (which means Krakow in Yiddish). Other Krakovian bands playing Jewish music include the Krakow Klezmer Band and the Polish-Ukrainian Zwierciadło (the Looking Glass). Their performances can be heard in ul. Szeroka in Kazimierz, whose restaurants hold Jewish music concerts nearly every night (*see p. 133*). The best opportunity to savour traditional Jewish music, however, comes during the Jewish Culture Festival (*see below*).

THE JEWISH FESTIVAL
(held annually in June/July)

"There is no Polish history without Jewish history or Jewish history without Polish history", says Konstantin Gebert, journalist and Judaist. This thought inspired two Poles, Krzysztof Gierat and Janusz Makuch, to launch a Krakow Jewish Festival in 1988, as a way of exploring the city's lost Jewish past and to analyse the common points of reference of Polish and Jewish culture. In its first years the Festival was strictly unofficial, as a blanket Communist taboo had been thrown over any discussion of things Jewish in Poland. Since the fall of Communism, the Festival has gone from strength to strength, with performers, artists, musicians and speakers coming from all over the world to take part in a

festival, mainly of music, which culminates in an open-air concert in Szeroka. Every year the concert seems to be rained on - but never rained off. Szeroka is always filled to the brim with people singing, dancing, drinking kosher wine and eating traditional Yiddish food. Though he was not referring to Cracovian Jewry when he wrote it, Czesław Miłosz's poem *And Yet the Books* seems appropriate here:

And yet the books will be
there on the shelves,
separate beings
That appeared once, still wet
As shiny chestnuts under a tree in
autumn,
And, touched, coddled, began to live
In spite of fires on the horizon, castles
blown up...

Jewish Krakow, like the books, is being taken off the shelf of history and cherished once more by a new generation of young people who also feel that there is no complete history of Poland without its Jewish history.

CONTEMPORARY MUSIC

Krakow has produced a number of contemporary composers - Bogusław Schaefer, Marek Chołoniewski, Krystyna Moszumańska-Nazar and Marek Stachowski, and every May their works are performed during

the Krakow Composers Festival. The most famous contemporary composer of them all, however, is Krzysztof Penderecki (*see p. 66*), who extends his patronage over many musical events, including the annual Krzysztof Penderecki International Contemporary Chamber Music Competition in September.

OPERA

One thing cannot be disputed about Krakow's opera: it is performed upon one of the loveliest stages in Europe. Akin to the Viennese opera house, it is more compact and cosier, with its shaded boxes, plush seats, mirrors, and gilded edges. Arias

reverberate in the Słowackiego Theatre (*see p. 92*) on Sunday and Monday nights; for the rest of the week the venue hosts theatre and ballet performances. (*pl. Św. Ducha; box office open Mon, Fri, Sat 10am-1pm and 4pm-7pm; Tues, Wed, Thur 1pm-6pm, Sun 12 noon-7pm*).

JAZZ

Jazz is alive in Krakow all year round. Check out the Harris Piano Jazz Bar (Rynek 28), Kornet (Al. Krasińskiego 19), U Muniaka (Floriańska 3), Piec Art (Szewska 12) or Indigo (Floriańska 26) for live performances. Keep your ears open for local jazzmen, too: Jarosław Śmietana, Mr Bober's Friends, the Old Metropolitan Jazz Band, or the Boba Jazz Band. Again, there's a profusion of jazz festivals: Jazz Juniors in April, The Old and the Young, or Jazz in Krakow in May, the Krakow Jazz Festival and Summer Jazz Festival at Piwnica pod Baranami (Rynek Główny 27) in July and August, the Miles Davies Memorial in September, and the All Souls' Day Jazz Convention in November.

Live music at Stalowe Magnolie (Steel Magnolias, Św. Jana 15) varies

Roma musician busking in the Rynek.

The Marksman King in all his glory.

from jazz to soul to soft rock. Other live music venues include LaBB (pl. Nowy 8) and Antykwariat (Dietla 75). Solid rock and other live concerts can be found at Miasto Krakoff (Łobzowska 3), Pod Jaszczurami (Rynek Główny 8), Klub 38 (Budryka 4), or Rotunda (Oleandry 1). Cracovian names to watch out for include Maanam, Świetliki, Maciej Maleńczuk, Renata Przemyk, Paulina Bisztyga, or the Motion Trio of three accordions.

FOLK MUSIC

Poles' interest in their folk traditions was, as in so many countries across the region, badly damaged by the banality of Communist "fakelore", which hijacked traditional tunes and dances as the ideal sort of good, clean fun that labouring Jacks and Jills should be having in their free time. In the 19th century, however, Polish traditional dances had swept the ballrooms of Europe. The Mazurka and the Polonaise were both traditional country dance rhythms popularised among the gentry and the aristocracy, largely by the music of Chopin. The Polonaise originated as a slow folk dance, and came to be associated with weddings, as an expression not of the joy and merriment, but rather of the serious, solemn side of the occasion - the bride leaving her parents' roof and saying goodbye to carefree girlhood forever. Krakow has a traditional dance of its own, too, the *Krakowiak*, more energetic than the Polonaise, set to a two-beat rhythm which puts you quite quickly out of breath.

Gypsy music is not a large part of Polish musical life, though you will find Roma ensembles in most of the larger towns.

INLAND SEA SONGS

Maybe it was nostalgia for an absent ocean that spawned the Krakow Sea

Shanty Festival, which ebbs and flows here every February. And every Friday of the year, live sea shanties are played at the Stary Port (Old Port) Tavern (*Straszewskiego 27*).

Information about most concerts and events can be obtained, and tickets bought, from the Cultural Information Centre at Św. Jana 2. Open Mon-Fri 10am-6pm, Sat 10am-2pm. Tel: 421-77-87, www.karnet.krakow2000.pl

FESTIVALS & CELEBRATIONS

Cracovians love any opportunity for a celebration, and no matter when you come to town, you are almost sure of stumbling upon a festival - of music, theatre, film, or dance - or even of prize pooches in the 30-year-old Dachshund Parade, in memory, perhaps, of the first ever Cracovian sausage-dog, which belonged to the great innovator Zygmunt the Old. The parade was viewed askance by Communist authorities who thought it must be meant as a parody of May 1st Labour Day parades. Carrying the Red Flag on Labour Day is no longer obligatory, but the Dachshund Parade lives on (a double victory of the underdog).

RELIGIOUS CELEBRATIONS

As a devoutly Catholic city, local town of the present Pope, you would expect Krakow to put on a wonderful show at Christmas and Easter. The first weekend of December sees a competition of Christmas cribs: nativity scenes in all the churches across town, with the cream of the crop on show in the Historical Museum. On Christmas Eve the Franciscan friars perform a nativity play outside their monastery.

Easter is a mixture of pagan and Christian ritual, with Easter baskets containing woolly lambs (symbol of Christ's sacrifice) and painted eggs (symbol of spring: rebirth and renewal). On Easter Monday the old village tradition of *śmigus dyngus*, where the boys throw buckets of water at the girls, takes to the streets with a vengeance.

OTHER FESTIVALS

In early summer, eight days before Corpus Christi, the colourful and noisy *Lajkonik* pageant parades through the town. Setting off from the Premonstratensian Convent in

Zwierzyniec, it follows the streets of Kościuszki and Zwierzyniecka to Franciszkańska, pl. Wszystkich Świętych, Grodzka and Rynek. The triumphant procession of the man-horse *Lajkonik* – or Zwierzyniec Pony – commemorates the victory over the Tartars in the Middle Ages, hence the man-horse's "Mongolian" costume. On Midsummer Eve (23rd June), the shortest night of the year, wreaths (*wianki*) are cast upon the waters of the Vistula. This ancient pagan ritual has been supplemented recently with modern pagan rituals such as open-air concerts, fireworks displays, and beer stalls.

Marksmen's fraternities, or shooting clubs, were a mediæval tradition across Europe, their aim being to train townsmen how to handle weapons in case of enemy attack. The Krakow Marksmen's Fraternity (*Bractwo kurkowe*) is 700 years old. The title of Marksman King – the best shot of all – is still the coveted prize in a centuries-old contest. The enthronement of the Marksman King, or the "King of the Cock" (*Król kurkowy*), takes place every June, when members of the Fraternity parade through town in period costumes.

KRZYSZTOF PENDERECKI (b. 1933)

Penderecki studied at the Krakow College of Music, where he worked as a teacher from 1958. He first came to prominence in 1959, when he won all three prizes at the Polish Composers' Festival. His music juxtaposes strange noise and sound colours with glissando and vibrato techniques. In the early 60s he turned to big vocal-instrumental works, using oratorio, opera and church music to great effect. His use of experimental compositional techniques in traditional musical forms is perhaps the secret of his popularity and success. In 1996 a performance of his piece *Seven Gates of Jerusalem*, commissioned by that city, formed part of the "Jerusalem - 3000 Years" celebrations.

RELIGIOUS MONUMENTS

The first dynasty to rule Krakow, the Piasts, was also the dynasty who Christianised it. The origins of the dynasty date from the 10th century, when six pagan tribes united to form one single people, the Polani, ruled by members of a quasi-mythical family, the Piasts. From the outset these Polani or Poles were forced to struggle against encroaching Germans from the west, Prussians from the north, and Bohemians and Magyars from the south. The first of the Piasts, Mieszko I (c.960-992) converted to Christianity in 966, swearing allegiance to the Pope in Rome, and firmly allying the country with the Western Church as opposed to the Church in Constantinople. A century later Bolesław the Bold (1058-1079) further cemented his ties with Rome by routinely supporting the Pope whenever he clashed with the Holy Roman Emperor - support which the Pope was unable to reciprocate when Bolesław was later accused of murdering his Bishop (*see p. 9*). The last ruler of the Piast line, Kazimierz the Great (1333-70), established the Krakow Academy in

Shadow of an ancient cross on ul. Szpitalna.

1364. In those days any academic institution wishing to become a fully-fledged university had to be granted the right to run a Theology Department. This right was granted by the Pope in 1400 and the Krakow Academy became the Jagiellonian University.

During the Counter Reformation, which raged across Catholic Europe in the late 16th and early 17th centuries, Krakow struck a singular note of tolerance. Under King Stefan Batory (1575-1586), himself a Protestant Transylvanian, the country remained Catholic, but the king declared that religious freedom was to be observed throughout his dominions, and passed an act of parliament forbidding violence to be used against non-Catholics. The Jesuits came to Krakow in 1582, and raised an Il Gesù-type Baroque church of great beauty, but they did not carry out any inquisitorial tortures nor burn any heretics at the stake. At the end of the century there were attempts to reunite the Greek Orthodox Church in Poland with the Catholic Church in Rome, a move which was unsuccessful, and which led to the formation of the Uniate Church, which uses the Eastern liturgy but bows to Papal authority.

N.B. Wawel Cathedral, the city's most important religious monument, is included in the Major Sights section on p. 21. Religious monuments listed below can be located from the Map References on pp. 156-157.

St Adalbert's Church
Rynek.
St Adalbert's is one of the oldest Romanesque churches in the city, built in the 11th century, before the Rynek Square itself, on which it stands. As the huge square was slowly paved over, the church began to sink, and has plunged three metres over the intervening centuries. St Adalbert, to whom the church is dedicated, was Czech-born, and had proselytised all over Central Europe before he made a start on the Prussians. He was killed in the attempt and his remains brought to Poland, where they were enshrined.

The Basilica Church of St Mary
(See also pp. 34-5.)
pl. Mariacki.
Like much in Krakow, this church has absorbed the styles of various ages and centuries. Originally a Romanesque stone basilica, which was probably destroyed during the Tartar invasion in 1241, it then

The Jesuit church of SS. Peter and Paul, seen from Wawel Hill.

bloomed as an early Gothic brick basilica. Its rib cross vaults effortlessly sustain the pointed roof. Apart from its twin towers and much fêted bugler (*see p. 35*), the church is also celebrated for its gorgeous polychrome wall decoration by Jan Matejko, Krakow's most famous Historicist artist (*see p. 54*). The prize possession of the church is the high altar by Veit Stoss, dedicated to the Virgin. Three-dimensional figures, muscles clenched, faces strained and grieved, support Mary in a heroic and beautiful piece of soft-wood sculpture made in the last decades of the 15th century by one of the great-

est of all the mediæval European sculptors (*see p. 77*).

THE FRANCISCAN CHURCH
Franciszkańska.

This church is most famous, perhaps, for its interior decoration by Wyspiański (*see p. 53*). The artist brings a whole exuberant world of meadow flowers into the pure forms of the Gothic interior. Below the blue firmament clad with golden stars, all the roses, nasturtiums, meadow lilies, pansies, sunflowers, irises, water lilies, dahlias, as well as an abundance of geometric and arabesque patterns, create a breathtaking interior, filled with joy and aesthetic harmony. The stained glass windows in the choir, also by Wyspiański, show Blessed Salomea, and St Francis receiving his Stigmata. Look behind you, and you will see the most powerful window of all: God the Father, caught in the very moment of creation, exclaiming "Let there be Light!", and depicted as God the Alchemist, a flame rising from the waters to create gold from dross. Dynamic and powerful, the window is reminiscent of the visions of Michelangelo and William Blake. Planets are born and fall out of God's cloak. In his attire, you will spot a very Cracovian motif, too: peacock feathers from a regional folk costume. The ornamental waves, so harmonised in colour, evoke a sense of the immensity of the universe and the primaeval ocean at the dawn of time. Everything is in motion, and the changing colours are most beautiful at sunset, when the varied hues of blue and purple succeed each other in the failing light. In the main nave, on your right as you stand with your back to the altar, past the stalls, is the Chapel of the Passion, belonging to the High Brotherhood of Our Lord's Passion, the only such fraternity in Poland, derived from the Mediterranean tradition. Clad in black cloaks and pointed hoods,

they bring the shudder of the Counter Reformation to Lenten ceremonies. Opposite the chapel is a painting of St Maximilian Kolbe, a Franciscan monk who was murdered in Auschwitz and beatified by the present Pope. The background shows his prisoner's stripes with his serial number in the lower right of the picture. In the right arm of the transept, you will see a door. If you find it open, go through it to enter the beautiful Gothic cloister. There you will see a portrait gallery of Krakow's bishops, from the 15th century up to the present. Among the murals is St Francis receiving his Stigmata and Christ in the Mystic Wine Press, which renders the notion of his "Real Presence" at the Eucharist very literally.

St. Katherine's Church
(Kazimierz, on the corner of Skałeczna and Augustiańska).
Founded by Kazimierz the Great for the Augustinian monastery, this church was built between 1345 and 1378. Impressive as it is, for reasons unknown it is over 12 metres shorter than originally planned. Twice damaged by earthquakes, and slated for demolition by the Austrians in the 19th century, St Katherine's has survived both natural and political foes. Its slender proportions and pil-

lar buttresses create the most translucent Gothic interior in Krakow, dazzling in its purity and might. Especially interesting are the mediæval murals in the cloisters, the main altar with the mystical *Marriage of St Katherine*, and the chapel of St Monica (patron saint of married women), also known as the Hungarian Chapel because its founder was the leader of a mercenary division in the Hungarian army. Next to the building's presbytery, right at the junction of Augustiańska and Skałeczna, stands a brick and timber belfry dating back to the 15th century.

THE OLD SYNAGOGUE
Kazimierz, Szeroka 24.

A Gothic mid 15th-century foundation, which after a great fire in 1557 was rebuilt by a Florentine, Matteo Gucci, in the Renaissance style. It was then that the women's prayer room was added on the northern side. The architect did not stick entirely to Renaissance principles, however. He introduced a ribbed vault in the central hall, perhaps in deference to the traditionalism of the community here. The synagogue was plundered, used as a warehouse, and partly destroyed in World War II. It has since been restored, and now

The interior of St Mary's with wall decoration by Jan Matejko.

houses a museum tracing the culture and history of the community who used it (*see p. 103*).

REMUH SYNAGOGUE
Kazimierz, Szeroka 40.
Named after Reb Moses Isserles (Remuh for short), the son of the synagogue's founder, the Remuh was built in the mid 16th century on the remains of a previous wooden structure destroyed, like the Old Synagogue, by the fire of 1557. This is a working synagogue with its own wailing wall: on the eastern wall of its cemetery, gravestones that were desecrated during the Nazi occupation have now been embedded. Reb Moses' tomb survives, as it was covered with earth by the congregation in 1939, as were other important tombs. Reb Moses' tomb is usually covered with scraps of paper, left by visitors from all over the globe, who place prayers and wishes on his grave (*see also p. 102*).

CHURCH OF SS. PETER AND PAUL
pl. Św. Marii Magdaleny.
When the Jesuits arrived in Krakow in 1582, determined that Rome's sway over the Polish church should remain unshaken, they adopted the theatrical Baroque style as the best way of asserting their presence. This church was built for them. It was the first Baroque church in Krakow, and is also the largest church in the city. Begun at the turn of the 17th century, it was completed in 1619 by Giovanni Trevano of Lugano, an Italian architect employed by the Polish king Zygmunt Vasa. Krakow's Jesuit church is one of the most faithful adherents to the model of the famous Il Gesù Church in Rome. The influence of the Counter Reformation can be seen in its monumentality of form, coupled with a certain coldness and austerity in the interior. It was erected on the Latin cross plan with a spacious nave designed to hold a large congregation of followers. The fine stuccoes inside the church are the work of another Italian artist, Giovanni Battista Falconi. The black marble altars and tombs seem minute against the massive columns and pillars. The decoration of the church is composed of motifs glorifying the Jesuits and King Zygmunt. The notion of an understanding between the Eastern and Western churches, which the Jesuits wanted to promote in Poland, is reflected in the dual dedication of the church: St Peter was the first Pope (in the West) and St Paul was the Apostle of the East.

In the chancel crypt lies Piotr Skarga, an outstanding Polish preacher and political writer. On his

*Renaissance interior of the
Isaac's Synagogue.*

tombstone you will see many mysterious little sheets of paper. They are wishes left here by locals, as Skarga is believed to provide help in passing exams, driving tests and other equally tiresome matters.

ISAAC'S SYNAGOGUE
Kazimierz, ul. Izaaka.
Opened in 1644, after wrangles with the local Christian community (*see p. 106*), this synagogue caused a sensation for being 14 metres high. The prayer hall has a barrel vault and lunettes, with a delicately arcaded women's section upstairs. The stucco work was superbly executed by an Italian, Giovanni Battista Falconi. The old story goes that a group of local thieves, hearing of the treasures the synagogue possessed, had decided to raid it. Kazimierz is a very small place, though, and word of what was afoot soon got out. A wise old rabbi ordered 26 of the local brave and true to dress in ritual death-shifts, arm themselves with clubs, and lurk in the neighbouring Remuh cemetery, which is where the rabbi was sure the thieves would make their entry, jumping over the cemetery wall that separated the Jewish enclave from the Christian area of the town. He was right. The thieves scaled the wall - and to their horror were confronted by legions of the dead, rising from their graves in white shirts. They scattered in panic, only to be clubbed by the "dead"

The Franciscan Church.

11th century, and it was there that Bishop Stanislaus was buried after his murder in 1079 (*see p. 9*), when he excommunicated King Bolesław The Bold who then - so the story goes - chopped his head off and threw his headless corpse into a pond outside. A Gothic church was then built to commemorate St Stanislaus, replaced in the 18th century by this two-storied late-Baroque church, designed by the architects Anthony Gerhard Münzer and Antonio Solari in 1733-42. Set in a garden, hidden behind the wall, the church and the adjoining Pauline monastery form a quiet, green island sheltered from the noise of the town. The defensive position of the site, next to the Vistula river, encouraged settlements as early as the 9th century, and the garden pond is believed to have been used for pagan sacrifices. After St Stanislaus' body sank into its waters, however, it was credited with heal-

who proved to be ghoulishly muscular. Today the synagogue is a museum, and has film showings of Jewish life in Krakow before World War II.

SKAŁKA CHURCH
Kazimierz, Skałeczna.

The first chapel of St Michael the Archangel on Skałka was built in the

ing powers for eye and skin diseases. A late Baroque statue of the Stanislaus rises from the middle of the pool. Many well-known Poles have been laid to rest in the church's Crypt of Honour, built in 1880. They include the 15th-century chronicler Jan Długosz, whose *Historia Polonica* charts the story of the nation from ancient times; and the Art Nouveau painter and poet Stanisław Wyspiański (*see p. 53*). Each year on 8th May, a ceremonial procession carries Saint Stanislaus' relics from Wawel Cathedral to Skałka.

THE UNIVERSITY CHURCH (ST ANNE)
Św. Anny.

The original Gothic church was replaced by the present Baroque one when the University authorities decided that a more prestigious and impressive building was required. The church was built and decorated between 1689 and 1703, based on a design by a Dutch architect, Tylman of Gameren. He had to compromise, as the construction site was bounded by the city walls, which were only pulled down in the 19th century. Because the church could not be built at the end of the street, on its axis, which would have been the most appropriate location, the architect carved the façade in deep relief and thus created rich contrasts of

light and shadow. The interior is the work of the Italian artist Baltasare Fontana, with frescoes by Karl Dankwart and the brothers Innocenzo and Carlo Monti. The *trompe l'oeil* is so effective that it is sometimes difficult to tell which column or statue is real and which is painted, while the rays of light entering the church only enhance the effect.

Among the crowd of saints and symbols, look under the dome for the personifications of the four Cardinal Virtues of Prudence, Temperance, Justice and Fortitude, seraphs and the Apocalyptic book of the Seven Seals (over the main nave), and the Revelation (over the choir). On the pillars are the twelve Apostles, painted *en grisaille*, and below the arcs you will find the twelve Sibyls, who entered the Christian tradition from Greek mythology.

In the right-hand transept is the tomb of St John of Kęty, also by Baltasare Fontana. St John of Kęty, or Jan Kanty (1390-1473), was a professor at the Jagiellonian University. One of the miracles that led to his beatification was his helping a little servant girl who had broken the milk jug she had been carrying. She was crying, fearing punishment from her mistress. Jan Kanty felt sorry for the child, and made the jug whole again, along with the milk inside it. On top of the columns surrounding his sarcophagus are the figures of four St Johns, predecessors of John of Kęty: St John the Baptist, St John the Evangelist, St John Chrysostom, and St John Damascene. The sarcophagus, containing the relics of the saint, rests on the arms of four figures which symbolise the faculties of the University: Law, Medicine, Philosophy, and Theology.

CONTEMPORARY CHURCHES

The inter-war period saw very little church building, and its immediate Communist aftermath none whatsoever. Demonstrations for religious freedom from the 1960s to the 1980s brought results, though, in the form of a spate of church building and some interesting designs. After World War II synagogues lay abandoned and stripped bare for half a century, until efforts began to be made to preserve them in the 1990s.

THE CHURCH OF OUR LADY OF CZESTOCHOWA
Nowa Huta, Al. Solidarnosci.

This church is one of several in Nowa Huta, the 1950s model workers' town (*see p. 121*). In 1961 the Nowa Huta steelworkers demonstrated, demanding freedom of conscience and the right to build churches. Stalinism had done little to knock Catholicism off the map in Poland, a fact which Solidarity understood very well when it started to gather momentum in the 1980s - Nowa Huta was one of its strongholds. This church, with its tent-like roof over the main entrance and explosion of Christian symbolism (there are even crosses on its drainpipes), was built in 1984-85, appropriately enough on Solidarity Street. The interior is light and airy, a clean and simple space with brick-ribbed arches that is very different from the monoliths of the original foundry town.

VEIT STOSS

Veit Stoss (c.1438-1533, known as Wit Stwosz in Polish) was born in Swabia, near Nüremberg. He is universally acknowledged as one of the most important late mediæval sculptors who ever lived. In his youth he was described as a "restless, unquiet citizen", and perhaps clashes with the authorities in Nüremberg induced him to renounce citizenship of the city and move to Krakow, where he set up a workshop and lived for almost twenty years. His masterpiece is the winged altar of the Dormition of the Virgin in St Mary's Basilica on the Rynek (*see p. 34*), carved in linden wood, and which he completed in 1477. In the centre Mary is seen sinking to rest into the arms of an Apostle, while the scene above shows her ascension to Heaven, to be crowned by God the Father and God the Son, while the patron saints of Poland, St Adalbert and St Stanislaus (*see p. 9*), look on. Every single one of the figures, every lock of hair, every furrowed brow and every strained sinew, was taken from life. Some have criticised the work for precisely this, for containing too much naturalism and not enough spirituality. Others disagree profoundly, arguing that it is precisely the altar's unabashed, warts-and-all realism that makes it so intimate and so arresting. Picasso called the work the eighth wonder of the world. Stoss was made an honorary citizen of Krakow, and exempted from city taxes. The tomb of King Kazimierz Jagiello in Wawel Cathedral was also designed by Stoss, though it is not certain that he carved it himself. In later life Stoss made peace with his native Swabia and returned to Nüremberg, where he died at a ripe old age.

PART III

GUIDED WALKS

Each of these walks is designed to take between 45 minutes to an hour. By visiting the museums, churches, cafés or restaurants that are included along the way, you can make them last a whole morning or afternoon.

Key streets and sights are marked in bold throughout. The itineraries of all four walks, in relation to the city as a whole, are shown on the map on p. 154.

Madonna on ul. Floriańska.

WALK ONE

WITHIN THE MEDIÆVAL CITY WALLS

This walk takes you within the mediæval walled city, taking in Krakow's main shopping street, its most celebrated museum, and wandering along the winding alleys where Joseph Conrad and Tadeusz Kantor once trod.

This walk starts with a morning coffee at **Camelot**, a favourite café with Cracovians. It lies in a little pocket of Św. Tomasza, known as "Doubting Thomas Lane" by the locals. Turn right into Tomasza, and then left into Floriańska, past the **Pod Różą Hotel**, one of the oldest in town. The Latin motto over its Renaissance portal reads: "May this house stand until an ant has drunk all the water in the sea, and a tortoise has walked around the globe". Tsar Alexander I and the composer Franz Liszt both stayed here, while today it

The Sukiennice (Cloth Hall) in the centre of the Rynek.

St Florian's Gate.

Floriańska you pass the longest section of the **mediæval city walls** still standing. Most of the walls were pulled down at the beginning of the 19th century, as they were in many cities across Europe, to make space for the growing metropolis. The surviving north fragment of the wall narrowly escaped destruction thanks to the arguments set forth by Professor Feliks Radwański of the Jagiellonian University. When historical arguments failed, he appealed to the reluctant City Senate by saying that, should the walls be pulled down, the northern winds would blow with "the utmost violence" through the city, threatening its inhabitants, particularly "ladies and children of delicate breeding" with frequent "flushes, rheumatic diseases, and perhaps even paralysis". Moreover, walking would be very difficult in such strong winds: "It would be a task of exceeding difficulty merely to remain on one's feet". Last but not least came the

boasts visiting state presidents and other important guests.

Continue down **Floriańska**. Now Krakow's main shopping street, it began life as a small section of a trade route leading from the Baltic to the Black Sea. The various quarters of the mediæval town traditionally belonged to different craftsmen's guilds that founded and maintained the gates in the defensive walls that encircled the city. At the very end of

threat of immodesty: just imagine what dreadful things would happen to the skirts of respectable ladies...

Pass through the gate to reach the Planty. When Krakow's fortifications were demolished, they were replaced by this green promenade (the name Planty derives from the word "plantations"), now useful in Krakow's ongoing battle against traffic pollution. Of the original 47 mediæval city towers (including eight tower-gates), only four have survived: Haberdashers' Tower (*Pasamoników*) to the east, Joiners' Tower (*Stolarska*) and Carpenters' Tower (*Ciesielska*) to the west, with the building of the Municipal Arsenal between them. The fourth, which closes off Floriańska, is **St Florian's Gate** (*Brama Floriańska*). It was built in the early 14th century as a safeguard against Ottoman invasion, and was then connected to the outer building of the Barbican located behind it by a narrow neck. The Barbican had seven turrets and two storeys with arrow-slits, as well as what were known as murder holes, openings in the floor used for pouring boiling water or simmering pitch onto the enemy below.

After a glance at the Barbican, walk back under St Florian's Gate. Inside is a late Baroque copy of the miraculous icon of the Madonna of the Sands (the original can be found in the Carmelite Church in Karmelicka). She shares responsibility for protecting the city with St Florian (patron saint of Krakow and of firemen), and with the eagle from the Piast dynasty coat of arms, which is carved on the outside of the tower. The 17th-century inscription found inside the gate translates: "The eagle in the gate under towers three, With wide open wings, kind guest, welcomes thee. Whilst adjudging discreetly as the city's guard, Who shall be admitted and who debarred".

With the gate behind you turn right into **Pijarska**, where you will see an open-air art gallery. Art both low and high seems to be found on these walls: kitsch galore in the open-air gallery, and genuine masterpieces a mere stone's throw away. A few steps ahead of you, on either side of the bridge at the corner of Pijarska and Św. Jana, is the **Czartoryski Museum**, the oldest in Poland, and home to one of its greatest art treasures of all, Leonardo da Vinci's *Lady with an Ermine* (*see p. 50*).

Right next to the Czartoryski Museum is Francesco Placidi's **Piarist Church**. Unlike mediæval churches, in which the east-west orientation was observed, churches in the Baroque period were carefully fitted into the space available. This is a perfect example of Baroque town planning. Three storeys high, crowned with an open bell tower, it dominates the street.

The Piarist order settled in Krakow in the second half of the 17th century. Initial work on the church was carried out between 1718 and 1728 by Kasper Bażanka (see p. 45), while the façade, completed in 1759, is entirely the work of Placidi. The impressive interior is completed with frescoes, which open the vaulting to the heaven of Baroque saints. The artist, Franz Eckstein, was influenced by Andrea Pozzo's work in the S. Ignazio church in Rome. It was during the Baroque period, in fact, that Krakow earned the soubriquet "Little Rome": never before or since have so many grand churches been built in the city. The crypt is used during Easter Week (notably on Good Friday) to display a model of Christ's Tomb, always very elaborate and usually including allusions to contemporary life and current politics. During the Solidarity years the Tomb was used as a vehicle for linking the suffering of Christ with the sufferings of Poland.

Św. Jana street takes you to the **Rynek** (see p. 29), the biggest mediæval square in Europe. Cross it,

and go into Bracka. If you need a break, try the Prowincja café (on your right at No. 3). Owned by a famous Cracovian bard, Grzegorz Turnau, it serves good coffee and cakes, along with the thickest hot chocolate in town.

At the end of Bracka cross a street which marks the edge of the oldest mediæval settlement, formerly known as Okół. In front of you is the 13th-century **Franciscan Church** (see p. 69). The Friars of St Francis came to Krakow from Padua in 1237 and built a brick church, consecrated in 1269. It was here that the pagan Lithuanian Władysław Jagiello was baptised before being allowed to sit on the Christian throne of Poland. (see p. 24) The church was damaged by the great fire of Krakow in the summer of 1850, a disaster which ultimately provided scope for the creative meeting of styles you see today. The interior was redecorated by Stanisław Wyspiański, the most distinguished Cracovian artist of his time (see p. 53).

Leaving the church with its main portal behind you, you will see the **Bishops' Palace** on your right. This is where Pope John Paul II always stays during his visits to Krakow. Alas, he can never get much sleep, as many Cracovians are so overcome with joy at his presence

Sculptured enclosure outside the church of SS. Peter and Paul.

that they serenade him under his window around the clock.

The little square where you are now standing has witnessed many dramatic scenes. It is here that Władysław Łokietek (the Elbow-High) hid from the Silesian prince Henryk Probus in 1289. The two men were rivals to the throne, and though Probus had the upper hand at first, the pint-sized Łokietek bade his time, and was eventually the first king actually to be crowned in Krakow (1320). In 1289, however, when fate was still against him, he had to ask the Franciscans to help him escape the city in disguise. According to the legend, he then hid in a limestone grotto near the city, in what is now the Ojców National Park. The story goes that a friendly spider swiftly spun a web across the entrance to Łokietek's hiding place, so that if Probus' men found it they would assume that no one had recently entered or left it.

Princess Jadwiga (*see p. 48*) is also connected with this square. She is said to have met her beloved prince Wilhelm Habsburg in the cloister here, before she decided to sacrifice her love *pro publico bono*, marry the swarthy Lithuanian, the much older Jagiello, and secure the throne of a joint kingdom. She become a saint for her pains.

Go straight ahead to the garden wall now, and pass through the gap. In front of you is the building of the Krakow Philharmonic Hall. Turn left to follow the Planty until you come to ul. Poselska, at which point turn left once more. To the right is the entrance to a lovely garden, opening onto the handsomest **view of Wawel Castle** from anywhere in Krakow. This is the Archaeological Museum (*see p. 55*). In front of you, on the left hand side of the street, there is a large municipal building, **Poselska 12**. On its façade there is a plaque which reads: "Around 1860, in a house that stood on this site, lived the son of a wandering poet, Józef Konrad Korzeniowski - Joseph Conrad. He brought the Polish soul to English letters". There is also a quote from Conrad himself, which reads: "It was in that old royal and academic city that I ceased to be a child, became a boy and came to know the friendships, the admirations, the thoughts and the indignities of that age". Conrad visited Krakow only once more, in 1914, when he saw the city flooded with moonlight, and populated with shadows from the past.

At the edge of the Archaeological Museum turn right down Senacka

which twists left to meet **ul. Kanonicza**, acclaimed as the most beautiful street in Krakow. Its name derives from the canons of Krakow Cathedral. It twists dreamily and unhurriedly off to the right, towards Wawel Castle. It is a street that keeps its secrets and treasures well guarded, though if you look closely at its portals, peep into its inner courtyards, climb its stairs, and descend into its cellars you will still find some traces of them. At No. 5 is **Cricoteka**, former studio of avant-garde artist and theatre-maker Tadeusz Kantor (*see p. 38*).

Instead of making for Wawel (*see p. 19*), turn left, going through Plac Marii Magdaleny into Grodzka. Before you rises the **Church of SS. Peter and Paul**, the first Baroque church in Krakow, commissioned for the Jesuits at the beginning of the 17th century. The façade of the church was set back, with a small courtyard in front. Between 1715 and 1722, Kasper Bażanka (*see p. 45*) fenced it in with a monumental enclosure consisting of the figures of the twelve Apostles. The present figures are replicas of the 18th-century originals. Two of the statues were sponsored by Pope John Paul II himself.

Next door to SS. Peter and Paul is the much smaller Romanesque

Church of St Andrew. Along with St Adalbert's on the Rynek, this is one of the only two Romanesque churches still extant in the city. St Andrew's embodies the transition from a severe mediæval interior to the ornate and prolix spirit of the Baroque era. Particularly fine is the Rococo pulpit, symbolically representing the boat of St Peter, fisherman of souls. The outside walls look more like the ramparts of a fortress. Indeed, the church is believed to have survived the Tartar invasion in the 13th century, with citizens hiding inside for protection.

Opposite, at No. 53, is the **Collegium Iuridicum**, one of the earliest of the University buildings, and now home to the Art History department. Step into the arcaded courtyard and admire the lovely sculpture there. It is for you to decide: is it the face of a sleepy girl, an ancient goddess, or perhaps a Buddha? This building also houses a tiny museum of shells and butterflies.

If you are hungry take the first street to the right – you are now back in Poselska, the street of restaurants. After about 100 metres you can whisk yourself away to the island of Sardinia (Corleone at No. 19) or to Corsica (Paese at No. 24). Or you can take a journey on the Orient Express (at No. 22) - but don't forget to book one of the plush train banquettes in advance.

Statue in the Collegium Iuridicum.

NICOLAS COPERNICUS
(1473-1543)

When Copernicus published his *On the Revolutions of the Heavenly Spheres* in 1543, the year of his death, admirers exclaimed that he "stopped the sun and moved the earth". Others, putting it more prosaically, claim that modern science had begun. Copernicus studied at the Krakow University between 1491 and 1495, going on to study further at Bologna and Padua. In 1513 he first formulated his heliocentric theory: the sun and not the earth is the centre of the universe, and the earth revolves around a stationary sun. Because his ideas were in direct contradiction to the Book of Joshua, Copernicus was nervous about bringing his book before a wider public lest the Church place an interdiction on it, and only circulated his manuscript among fellow scientists. In the decades that followed, however, he gained wider support, including that of Pope Paul III, who in fact urged him to publish. Perhaps the Pope regarded the work as no more than the foolish fancy of an amateur star-gazer. Martin Luther certainly did, calling Copernicus a "fool" for trying to "reverse the science of astronomy" and disprove holy writ. During Copernicus' lifetime his theory remained no more than a hypothesis. With the invention of the telescope, however, somewhere around 1600, it was conclusively proved to be true, and caused enormous ructions in academic and religious circles - a furore that Copernicus never lived to see. Memorabilia from Copernicus' time in Krakow can be seen in the Jagiellonian University Museum (*see p. 56*).

Facing Page: Detail of the Grunwald Monument in plac Matejki.

WALK TWO

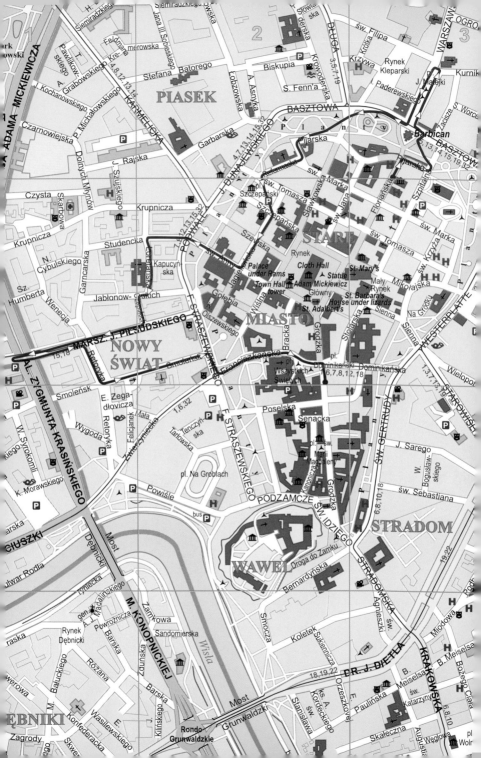

AROUND THE PLANTY

This walk covers the west part of the Planty, a green belt that girdles the old city, taking in a wealth of imposing late 19th-century buildings, including the beautiful Słowackiego Theatre.

Enjoy a coffee among amazing artworks in **Jama Michalika** at Floriańska No. 45, established in 1895 (*see p. 136*). On a sunny morning your eyes may take a moment to adjust to the dimly lit, fin-de-siècle interior. A century ago it was the favourite hang-out of artists from the nearby Fine Arts Academy, as well as of poets, journalists, philosophers, and all sorts of café society hangers-on. Its literary cabaret the "Little Green Balloon" made smug fun of the bourgeois, conservative lifestyles of local burghers. On the way out, look out for the distorted, distinctly

The green ring of the Planty turns gold in October.

inebriated-looking painting, *St Florian's Gate*, with a green balloon floating above it, all twisting and wobbling in this drunken vision of the painter Szczygliński, who is said to have painted it after a festive night at the Cabaret. When you walk out of the café, turn right, and you will see the original **St Florian's Gate** (*see p. 82*).

Walk towards the gate and turn right just before you get there. You will see the ornate sugar-plum pile of the **Słowackiego Theatre**, recalling the grand opera houses of Paris and Vienna. The building is the work of the architect Jan Zawiejski, who studied in Vienna and was clearly inspired by its Baroque beauty. Built in 1891-93, its richly ornamented façade has allegorical figures of Music, Opera, Operetta, Poetry, Drama, Comedy and two heroes from Mickiewicz's *Pan Tadeusz* (*see p. 36*): Tadeusz and Zosia, about to dance the Polonaise, as well as the lofty inscription *Kraków narodowej Sztuce* (Krakow's gift to national art). Its interior, true to its façade, boasts an abundance of mirrors, gold, and red plush, and a lovely - if bombastic - curtain. The theatre was erected on the site of the mediæval Monastery of the Holy Spirit. By 1885 the monastery buildings were so dilapidated that instead of repairing them, the City Council decided to pull them down, to the outrage of painter Jan Matejko (*see p. 45*). Matejko - a freeman of the city of Krakow - mounted a protest, but to no avail. Bitterly disappointed and hurt, Matejko renounced his honorary citizenship; and some say that he even put a curse on the place where the theatre was to stand.

Hidden behind the theatre is the small Gothic **Church of the Holy Cross**. At the turn of the last century, the architects Stryjeński (*see p. 45*) and Hendel and the painter Wyspiański (*see p. 53*) worked on the church's restoration. The beautiful Gothic vaulting opens up like a fan from a single central pillar. Jan Matejko was christened in the Gothic baptistry; among the epitaphs is a 1909 plaque commemorating the actress Helena Modrzejewska - but more of her later.

Double back to the left now, and head around the outside of the remaining walls into the **Planty ring**, a great green swathe in the middle of town, for which the town paid a high price: the loss of its mediæval city walls (*see p. 83*). The Planty was modelled on Vienna's Ringstrasse and, just like in Vienna, many important buildings were constructed here, including the imposing

The exuberant façade of the Słowackiego Theatre.

building of the **Academy of Fine Art**, which you will see on your right in plac Matejki behind the Barbican. Jan Matejko, after whom the square is named, was the first director of the Academy; throughout its history, the institution has educated a host of famous names, including Andrzej Wajda (*see p. 58*) and Tadeusz Kantor (*see p. 38*).

In the middle of plac Matejki, opposite the Barbican, is the expressive **Grunwald Monument**, commemorating the victory of Polish troops led by King Władysław Jagiello against the Teutonic Knights at the Battle of Grunwald in 1410, an important victory as it helped secure Poland's access to the Baltic. The monument was erected to commemorate the 500th anniversary of the battle, on the initiative of the composer Paderewski.

At the north end of plac Matejki is **St Florian's church**, founded here because, so the story goes, the oxen drawing a cart containing St Florian's reliquary stopped here and stubbornly refused to move. In the chronicles the relics of this patron saint of firemen were brought to Poland in 1184 by Prince Kazimierz the Just. Ironically the church was damaged by many fires, but apparently St Florian himself, who is also one of the patron saints of Krakow, personally came down from heaven to help quench the flames in 1528. The present church is largely the result of 17th century reconstruction.

Go back down to the Planty and turn right, following the gardens until they are crossed by a road with a taxi stand. At the corner of Basztowa and Długa you will see the former **Chamber of Commerce and Industry** (now the headquarters of a literary publishers). Known as the House under the Globe (you only have to look up to see why), it was designed by Franciszek Mączyński, the most productive architect of fin-de-siècle Krakow (*see p. 46*).

Follow the Planty, taking a sharp turn left into Św. Marka, and then turn right into Reformacka, a street which takes its name from the 17th-century Reformati (Reformed Franciscan) Monastery and **Church of St Kazimierz**. The painting of Christ entombed in the Chapel of Christ the Merciful is believed to be miraculous. The Christ from the painting is said to have joined the monks at prayer during the great plague of 1707: when the litany ended he cried out "enough", and thus stopped the pestilence. In the crypt, almost a thousand dead were laid to rest, both rich and poor: the benefactors of the order, the Wielopolski and Szembek families; monks of the order; and beggars who ended their lives in the monastery. A survivor of Napoleon's Moscow campaign knocked for admittance at the gates of the monastery in 1812. He died in its infirmary, and lies next to Countess Domicella Skalska, a converted sybarite who became a lay sister and bequeathed all her wealth to the monastery. The bodies are perfectly mummified: a curious phenomenon, only partially explained by the unique microclimate of the catacombs.

On the other side of the street are the **Stations of the Cross**, painted between 1814 and 1816 by Michał Stachowicz. On the wall is an epitaph of the painter's wife Małgorzata, who was said by Stachowicz's contemporaries to have "effectively poisoned his life with her ceaseless pestering". But he, like Christ, called out "enough" and dumped his insufferable spouse in a nunnery.

Reformacka leads into **pl. Szczepański**, a square that takes its name from the church of St Szczepan, destroyed when the Habsburgs fortified the city during the mid 19th century. At the corner of the square and ul. Reformacka is a 1936 skyscraper, a building that raised a storm in Krakow because of its overtly modern form, and the fact that a mediæval tenement house was destroyed in the construction process. The investor (the District

Savings Bank) had to pay a 100,000 złoty fine, which was put towards the construction of the National Museum. Interesting that modern American-style architecture was made to pay for Cracovian aspirations. In front of you is the back façade of Pałac Sztuki, the **Palace of Art** designed by Mączyński (*see p. 46*). The architect was very much impressed by new architectural theories coming from abroad, including the idea of the *Gesamtkunstwerk*, which represented a synthesis of miscellaneous disciplines, as well as unity of style and function. The Palace of Art, the best Cracovian

example of this attempted synthesis, is a simple and coherent form. The frieze around the building represents two potential courses of an artist's life: one of success, when the artist is crowned with laurel in the presence of the Muses and Pegasus, and the other showing the route through Pain and Despair to failure and a fruitless end. The sculptured busts are of artists famous at the time, including Stanisław Wyspiański (*see p. 53*) and Jan Matejko (*see p. 54*).

Head around the Planty side of the building and you can see a low plaque at the edge of the walkway marking the spot where the Baszta

Angels guard your steps at the restaurant Pod Aniołami.

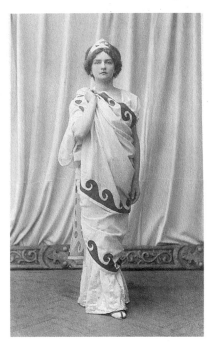

Celebrated actress Helena Modrzejewska.

USA and Great Britain with considerable success. Film director Andrzej Wajda has also directed many productions at the theatre, and continues to cook up new projects. In 1981 he invited actress Teresa Budzisz-Krzyżanowska to play Hamlet. The result was so good that Wajda was moved to proclaim her the best actor in Poland. The building also houses the Museum of the Old Theatre, and the Gaudíesque Maska Café, frequented by actors and their audiences. The café owner, Tadeusz Huk, is himself an actor at the theatre.

Turn right into Jagiellońska now, and walk on down it for two blocks until you reach Św. Anny. Turn right again, and return to the Planty. Cross over it and over ul. Podwale, and walk straight over into ul. Studencka, which contains many interesting 19th-century and turn-of-the-century tenement houses. Turn left into ul. Loretańska, with the red-brick 19th-century school building in a burgher style behind you. In Loretańska, on your right, is the **Capuchin Monastery** with the Church of the Annunciation and Loreto House, modelled on the Casa Santa in Loreto, the legendary dwelling of the Holy Family, said to

Garncarzy, one of the demolished mediæval towers, once stood. Opposite the main entrance to the Palace of Art is the Bunker of Art, built in the 1960s (*see p. 57*).

Walk down the side of plac Szczepański now, towards the Rynek. At the corner of Jagiellońska you will find **Teatr Stary** (the Old Theatre), built in 1903-6 (*see p. 46*). One of the many actors who trod the boards of the Stary Teatr is Helena Modrzejewska (now the theatre's patroness), a turn-of-the-century actress who emigrated to California. She was particularly known for her Shakespearian roles and toured the

have been brought there by air, in the arms of winged angels, from the Saracen-threatened Holy Land in 1291. In this Cracovian Loreto House Tadeusz Kościuszko (*see p. 48*) and his officers went to have their swords blessed before the 1794 National Uprising. In more recent times, Polish airmen have raised a plaque to the Blessed Virgin Mary of Loreto who, naturally enough, is the patron of large objects moving through the air. Note the new statue of Padre Pio to the left of the church entrance, basking in his new-found Papal approval.

Continue south now, crossing ul. Jabłonowskich, and entering Czapskich, which goes off a little to your right (both streets take their names from Cracovian noble families). Czapskich takes us to **Piłsudskiego**, the former Wolska – one of the main tracts leading westwards from the inner ring of the city, and now lined with imposing and grandiose buildings. Turn right into it. At No. 12 is a building which now belongs to the National Museum, the former home of the Czapski family, which now houses a numismatic collection from Vilnius. The pavilion has a clear inscription: *Monumentis Patriae Naufragio Ereptis* (To national mementoes saved from the shipwreck), and was designed by Stryjeński (*see p. 45*) and Hendel. One of the pillars of the fence supports a curious, crouching figure: a frog? A ram? Maybe a basilisk?

Piłsudskiego ends at the busy Al. Krasińskiego boulevard; on the other side of this lie the vast, refreshing green meadows of the **Błonia**. This is unusual given that it is such a short distance from the town centre - one might say it is still in the centre of town. These former wetlands of the Vistula and Rudawa rivers belonged to the city as early as the 15th century. The neighbourhood villagers were allowed to graze their cattle there - now the Błonia provides pasture for Cracovians, their dogs and an army of moles. A walk over the Błonia is a good option if you crave some contact with nature; culture cravers should head instead for **Retoryka**. Turn round, cross Al. Krasińskiego once more, go up Piłsudskiego, and take the first right into Retoryka to find a cluster of apartment blocks by Teodor Talowski (*see p. 47*). The very names of the houses: the House under the Singing Frog at No. 1, Festina Lente at No. 7, and the House under the Donkey (*Faber est suae quisque fortunae*: Everyone is the architect of their own fate) demonstrate the imagination and originality of the architect, and his knack for the picturesque. Fantasy mingles with reality and history - the House under the Singing

Frog once housed a music school, and overlooked the Rudawa river. The croaking frogs joined the chorus of students, and hence the house got its name.

Opposite, at No. 4, is the **House of a Hundred Balconies**, designed by Bohdan Lisowski and built between 1958 and 1961. Turn left into ul. Smoleńsk. On the right is the 17th-century **Church of Divine Mercy**, restored at the beginning of the last century. The name Smoleńsk is explained by a strange tale: once upon a time, a Jew by the name of Szmul met a poor scholar who tried to persuade him to be christened. Szmul laughed at him, saying: "when you become a bishop, then I will turn Christian". Years later the scholar did actually become a bishop. Szmul, seeing the hand of God at work, not only got himself christened but also founded the Church of Divine Mercy. The area, suburban at the time, was given the name of Smoleńsk to com- memorate the conversion of Szmul.

To the left, at No. 9, is the old Arts and Crafts Museum, built in 1908-1914, and now the Fine Arts Academy. At the end of the street, on either side, are two palaces. The one on the left is the former Wedding Palace (currently under restoration, and set to become a language school) while the one on the right is the Krakow Philharmonic Hall. Once upon a time one could be married and serenaded at the same time!

You are now back at the green girdle of the Planty. A good option for lunch or dinner is Pod Aniołami in Grodzka. (Continue across the Planty along Franciszkańska, which is to your right in front of the Philharmonic Hall. Go past the Franciscan church and the City Hall. Once past the City Hall, turn right into Grodzka, where the angels over Pod Aniołami will greet you at No. 35.)

Facing page: Screen in the Remuh Synagogue.

WALK THREE

JEWISH KAZIMIERZ

This walk takes you mainly through the old Jewish section of Kazimierz, once a separate town beyond the old city, and made famous in recent times by the filming of Schindler's List.

The mediæval town of Kazimierz was founded in the 14th century by King Kazimierz the Great (1333-1370), whose name it bears. The legend goes that the king had a beautiful Jewish mistress, Estera, with whom he had several children. Legend or no, Kazimierz did not found the town for her; he wanted to counterbalance the strong German influence in Krakow. In subsequent centuries, when pogroms in Bohemia, Italy, Spain and Germany were forcing Jewish communities to flee, they found sanctuary in Kazimierz. The town became famous for the diversity of Jewish traditions that thrived there. Krakow - and within it Kazimierz - became known as "the city and mother of Israel".

Enter the area from ul. Miodowa (trams 3, 24 from the Old Town)

Stained-glass menorahs in the Tempel Synagogue.

and leave the ugly 70s school behind you. Walk ahead, between a Jewish restaurant on the left and the old Landau's House building with its bookshop on the immediate right. Landau's daughter married the merchant Wolf Popper, founder of the Popper Synagogue, which you will come to later. Walk on into **Szeroka**, a huge street-cum-square that before the war was the centre of all trade in the Jewish town, as well as the seat of the Kahal. It is now the focal point of the Kazimierz Jewish Festival (*see p. 62*). Cross over the square to a wall that runs down to the **Remuh Synagogue**. A sign requests "do not walk on pavement this side as it is paved over graves on side of Remuh Synagogue". The wall contains the **Remuh graveyard**, one of the oldest in Europe. Some of its tombs bear ancient symbols: Stars of David and lions standing for the house of Judah; hands raised in blessing signifying the tombs of Kohens (rabbinical families); jugs and bowls on the tombs of Levites (assistants in the synagogue); crowns for scientists; snakes for doctors; and broken roses, signifying life cut off in its prime, on the graves of those who died young. Rabbi Moses Isserles (nicknamed Remuh), son of the synagogue's founder and famed for his wisdom and learning, is also buried

here. His grave is inscribed "From Moses the prophet to Moses Isserles, there never was such a Moses". His tomb is believed to possess special powers, and pilgrims from all over the world leave prayers and requests in the metal box on his grave.

There is a rabbi in Krakow today, though his community is a small one. The current Jewish population in Poland is much disputed, with estimates varying wildly between 3,500 and 25,000, though the reality is probably somewhere around 12,000. Certain Jewish rites and *minyan* services can only be held when there is a quorum of ten men, so in Kazimierz they happen rarely. The Remuh is the one working synagogue in Krakow, and has a congregation of fewer than 250 souls, most of whom are elderly. Originally wooden, the synagogue was destroyed by fire in 1557, after which the building you see now was constructed. A niche in the eastern recess is the place where Rabbi Remuh is said to have prayed.

Szeroka has three old synagogues in a space of about 100 metres, and there is also a **ritual bath house** - mikveh - at No. 6, dating from the 16th century (though rebuilt in the 19th), with the bath itself in a deep basement, close to the source of a natural spring. No. 14 is

Archive photograph of old Jewish Kazimierz.

the house where Helena Rubinstein was born, the daughter of a Jewish trader. At the age of 18 she was sent to visit her uncle in Australia, with 12 jars of cosmetic cream in her luggage. The cream, manufactured by a Cracovian Jewish dermatologist, launched a world-famous cosmetics empire.

A few doors down from the Remuh is the recently renovated **Popper Synagogue**, founded in 1620 by the merchant Wolf Popper, known as "the stork" from his habit of praying on one leg. Desecrated by the Nazis, the synagogue has now been restored (it now functions as an art gallery) and the restaurants serv-

ing Jewish-style food and drinks next door show how much the area has developed over the past decade.

At the southern end of Szeroka is the **Old Synagogue**, dating back to the mid 15th century. Originally built just for men, a prayer room for women was added in the late 16th century on the northern side. Inside there is a plaque dedicated to Tadeusz Kościuszko and the year 1795, when his National Uprising collapsed (*see p. 48*). He had called Jews to arms to help in the liberation of Poland, though his efforts were doomed to fail. On October 24th 1795, the Third Partition of Poland took place (*see p. 17*), with Russia

Old tram terminus on Św. Wawrzyńca.

taking what remained of Lithuania and the Ukraine, Prussia grabbing Mazovia and Warsaw, while Austria obtained the Krakow region.

During World War II the Old Synagogue was used as an army warehouse by German troops, but now it is full of sacred objects once again and has signs in English explaining the Jewish festivals. You'll find a display of beautiful beaded *yarmulkes* and of traditional Polish costumes. Upstairs there is an exhibition of oil paintings and photos, including one of Amon Goeth, the commander of Płaszów Camp, not far from the Nazi-created ghetto (*see p. 107*) in 1943.

On leaving the Old Synagogue, walk up the steps and double back along the raised section of Szeroka to your left where it continues as ul. Bartosza, and pass plac Bawół. This takes its name from the mediæval village, the centre of which was Plac Nowy, and which later merged with Kazimierz. Go on down to Św. Wawrzyńca, at which point turn right. Walk down it, cross ul. Wąska with its ruined tenements and school, and further on on your left you will see the **Museum of Municipal Engineering**, and to the right some old wooden tram shelters, which now function as a "Motodrom" for go-kart racing. The clock over the sheds, however, has long since given up going so fast!

Further on you come to the **Corpus Christi Church**, founded in 1340, by Kazimierz the Great. You have now left Jewish Kazimierz and have entered the old Christian part of the quarter. Corpus Christi's severe late Gothic exterior belies a richly ornamented interior revelling in gilding and wood carving. It is here that the Florentine architect of Renaissance Wawel, Bartolomeo Berecci, was buried in 1537, after his mysterious murder (*see p. 45*). Walk anti-clockwise round the outside of the church, and you will come to the **Gethsemane Chapel**, a cage full of Gothic sculpture, the only surviving part of the former graveyard. Leave it by the gate opposite the Małopolski Bank. Turn right down Bożego Ciała, pass the hairdresser Carmen, and then right again down ul. Józefa with its fur shop and antiques. This part of the area is now flourishing, with new blocks of flats opposite a bar. Walk down for two blocks and peer down ul. Estery for a glimpse of the **Tempel**, a reform synagogue built in 1862 and peaceful now, its lengthy and furious debates with the Remuh's Orthodox congregations long forgotten. Carry on down Józefa, peering in at a grey gateway on your left to see tenement housing typical of the area before the war. Józefa 19 is the site of a university department, the Collegium Kazimierzowskie. Turn left down Jakuba and cut diagonally across the park to pass in front of Hotel Eden and onto ul. Ciemna. Turn left into ul. Lewkowa, until you catch sight of the Remuh Synagogue again, and the little stained-glass window workshop, with the spiked gate and barbed wire wall of the next-door Police Station. Come out into Szeroka once more, walk on the right-hand pavement past the tenements of Szeroka 1, and turn left into Miodowa, with the wooden fence of the Remuh cemetery peeling with old posters. Cross over Jakuba and carry on down past the business school advertising its professional qualifications on the right. On the left is the **Kupa Synagogue**. To get to its main entrance, turn left into ul. Estery - named after King Kazimierz's beautiful mistress Estera, perhaps - then left again down Warszauera, named after a doctor who worked in the Jewish poor hospice in the area. Half way down on your left is the synagogue, gorgeously renovated with new wrought iron doors. Funded by Kahal (congregation) funds, it became the Kupa or purse temple. At the back of its yard are the remains of an old wall which might have been part of the original Kazimierz town walls. Double back from the synagogue entrance and turn left onto ul. Kupa, past the metal sailing ship over the door of the Amber jewellery store, to approach the early Baroque **Isaac's Synagogue**. To get to it, turn left into ul. Izaaka. This synagogue was financed by quite different means: by a wealthy banker, Isaac Jakubowicz, though a Hassidic story about him asserts that he was in fact a poor man to whom vast riches appeared in a dream. He travelled far and wide in search of them, but returned home empty-handed, whereupon he found the treasure in his own oven. Modern Krakow pays tribute to him with a new bankomat and credit bank with a gabled roof opposite his synagogue. Jakubowicz founded the temple in 1638, but was opposed by the Prior of Corpus Christi, who deemed it too near the Christian church. Prolonged wrangling between the communities then delayed construction until 1644. No longer a working synagogue, it now houses an exhibition on Polish Jewry, where two short films are shown. One shows scenes from everyday life in pre-war Kazimierz; the other, impassively shot by a German cameraman, shows the removal of the Jews to the Podgórze ghetto (*see p. 107*).

Go straight down Izaaka now, and cross Estery to enter **plac Nowy**, the market square, with its central market building on your right. Ever since the middle ages, this square has been the heart of all commercial activity in the area. Where once there were butchers and cloth merchants, you will now find stalls of vegetables (on weekdays) and second hand clothes (on Sundays).

Cross over plac Nowy and turn left down ul. Meiselsa, named after Rabbi Meisels, who called the Jewish people of Kazimierz to rise up against the oppression of Poland in the 19th century. At No. 17 is the former Bet Midrash (prayer hall) of Bne Emunah, built in 1886. Today it has been transformed into the **Center for Jewish Culture**, not a community centre so much as a resource and study centre on Polish Jewry. Peer into the courtyards next door, all interlocking, with their balconies archways and gateways, and dominated by the Corpus Christi church spire. When filming *Schindler's List*, Spielberg used these courtyards to recreate the ghetto, although the ghetto was never located in Kazimierz - it was in the district of Podgórze, across the Vistula (*see below*). Turn right off Meiselsa into Bożego Ciała. You are leaving Jewish Kazimierz once again, and

A courtyard near the Jewish Centre with the tower of Corpus Christi in the distance.

passing through what was once a gate in the old walls that surrounded the enclave. Walk on, and on the corner of Miodowa and Bożego Ciała you will see a block of bright green, built in 1899, with plastered scrolls and ornament. Now a café, this is a simple, pleasant place to relax over a plate of excellent *pierogi* smothered in butter.

PODGÓRZE, THE GHETTO

The actual ghetto in Krakow was not in Kazimierz itself, although that is where Spielberg filmed it for *Schindler's List*. It was in the district of Podgórze, a working-class area where a great many Jews also lived. By the river, a part of the old ghetto wall is still standing, in the shape of Jewish gravestones. Oskar Schindler's actual factory is also in this area at ul. Lipowa No. 4. Cracovians are rather ambivalent about the *Schindler's List* effect. True, it focused attention on the city, and today you can go on *Schindler's List* walking tours and buy books about the film. On the other hand, the confusion of cinematic fiction and historical fact is highly problematic: Oskar Schindler has entered people's minds as a German businessman who saved many of Krakow's Jews. Undoubtedly he did, but the majority of Krakow's Jews were not saved. There were 1,200 names on his list and about 70,000 Jews in the city in 1939. The facts speak for themselves.

To get to Podgórze, take trams 3, 9 or 11 from the Sienna Gate in the old town, and get off at the first stop over the river. As you travel down you are following the same route that the Jewish population did when they were rounded up and brought here in 1941. Thousands of people were driven over the river in carts piled with all they could take with them. At plac Bohaterów Getta 18 there is a small museum, housed in the old Pod Orłem pharmacy, once owned by Tadeusz Pankiewicz, a Pole who sought permission to stay within the ghetto walls and managed, over the two years that the ghetto lasted, to help many of its inmates by smuggling them medicines, food and information. He was also a crucial witness to the massacres that took place here. It was here that people were herded into different groups and selections were made as to who was to remain and who was to be moved on to the concentration camps. The museum, opened in 1983, is a grim reminder of what took place, though nowadays, at last, people are beginning to look forward as well as back. As Rafel Schaarf, founder of London's *Jewish Quarterly* and himself a Cracovian Jew, says, it is important to stop viewing Krakow and its environs as the biggest Jewish cemetery in the world and to focus more on ways in which Polish and Jewish culture come together.

Old gravestones in the Remuh cemetery.

Walk Four

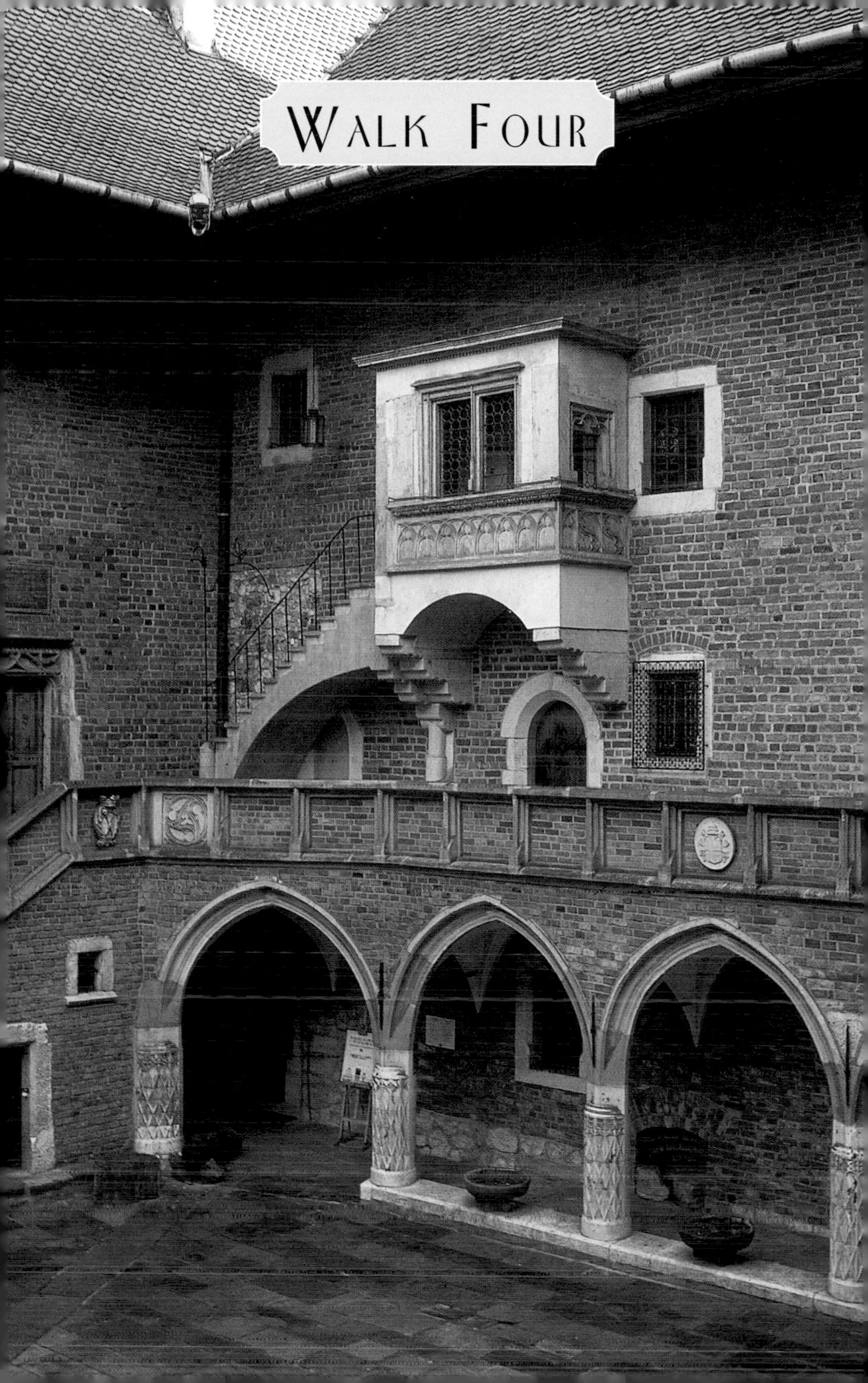

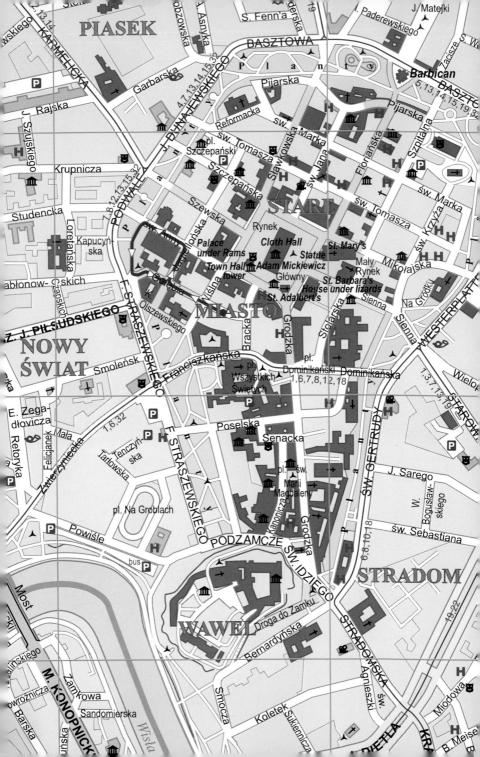

THE UNIVERSITY TOWN

This walk takes you round the Gothic and Renaissance quadrangles of the ancient Jagiellonian University, delving into halls where Copernicus studied and where alchemists and necromancers had their laboratories and seance tables.

From October to June, and even throughout the summer holidays, Krakow is a student town, home to the oldest university in Poland, founded in 1364. In addition, there are many academies, schools, conservatories and colleges turning out artists, poets, businessmen, dentists and nuclear physicists. This little stroll around the old university quarter starts in the **Mozaika Café** at Gołębia No. 5, a favourite haunt of members of academe both young and old. (If you cannot find a table in this small, cosy café, there are some good options next door: Café Gołębia 3, Gołębnik Tea Rooms, or Migrena Café.)

Gołębia means "pigeons" and an old graffito on the corner of Gołębia and Bracka mocks *"Ulica Gołębia dla*

Folk parade on ul. Gołębia. Previous page. Courtyard of the Collegium Maius.

gołębi" (Pigeons' Street is for pigeons!). If Krakow's pigeons had the vote, they would have less difficulty in forming a majority government than most of the existing political parties. Perhaps the only species to outnumber them are university students. They count for more than 10% of Krakow's population, and they are certainly visible. University professors, although not as numerous, have their say in every aspect of Cracovian life: their considered opinions are sure to appear in the local press whenever a new planet is discovered, plans for extending a road are discussed, or a new statue erected. Each year in May, the city celebrates the Juvenalia, when the Mayor hands the keys of the city over to the students. And if you happen to be in Krakow around the 1st of October, the chances are you will see a procession of Jagiellonian University professors in their gowns and mortar boards, walking through the University quarter to celebrate the start of the new academic year.

On leaving Mozaika, turn right, and cross Wiślna – you are now in a pedestrian area. On your left is the 15th-century **Collegium Opolskie**, which houses the Polish Philology Department. On your right is the back entrance to the 18th-century **Collegium Kołłątaja** (the old

Collegium Physicum). It was in this building, in 1883, that two Jagiellonian University professors, Karol Olszewski and Zygmunt Wróblewski, extracted liquid oxygen, and then nitrogen, for the first time. Kołłątaj himself was the father of educational reform at the Jagiellonian University (then called the Krakow Academy), and went on to become one of the authors of the first Polish Constitution (3rd May 1791). Today this college, connected by an inner courtyard and passage to Św. Anny, houses the Jagiellonian University Centre for Language Teaching and the University Archives.

At the corner of Gołębia and Jagiellońska, turn right into the latter, walk past the **Collegium Minus**, built in the 15th century, the seat of the first Art History faculty in Poland (established in 1882). Jan Matejko, first director of the Academy of Fine Art (*see p. 45*) studied here. The building is now home to the Jagiellonian University Institute of Archaeology.

The next building on your left is the **Collegium Maius**, the oldest surviving university building in Poland. It was founded in 1400, a year which marks the renewal of the University by King Władysław Jagiello, thanks to the legacy of his wife Jadwiga (*see p. 48*), a great benefactress and a recent addition to the pantheon of Catholic

Pious 19th-century portrait of
Queen Jadwiga.

departments of Theology
and the Liberal Arts and,
since 1450, a medical
school as well. The Medical
School now lives next
door.

Spacious and quiet,
Collegium Maius also has a
magical aspect. **Doctor
Faustus** (? - c.1538) is said
to have studied black
magic here. Although his
name does not appear in
the University records, it
appears in the testimonies
of his contemporaries. A
faithful researcher, Johann
Wolfgang von Goethe,
even visited Krakow in
1790, looking for traces of the
famous necromancer before writing
his *Faust*. Perhaps it was the artful
Doctor himself who conjured up
the spirit-image of Barbara
Radziwiłłówna, the much-mourned
wife of King Zygmunt August,
although other sources site that par-
ticular seance in Wawel Castle,
under the eagle eye of Master
Twardowski (*see p. 31*). Whatever
the case, the English alchemist John
Dee (1527-1608) also came to
Poland at the invitation of Olbracht

saints. Queen Jadwiga is said to have
donated all her jewels to the university, so she was buried in a wooden
necklace instead of a gold one.

Enter the Collegium Maius from
Jagiellońska. You will find yourself
in a spacious, late-Gothic arcaded
courtyard, with a well in the centre.
Originally the Collegium Maius
provided accommodation for the
professors, had a library upstairs
and a lecture hall downstairs: the
low-ceilinged, dark and often wet
lectoria. Later it came to house the

Old procession of Jagiellonian professors.

England. Dee left Krakow a mark of his presence: in 1584, he made a gift to the University Library of a manuscript of Boethius' *De Consolatione Philosophiae*, in which he inscribed his best wishes to the University of Krakow.

On leaving the courtyard, you will see the natural-stone outside wall, typical of the 14th century. It is made of limestone, the same material that the city walls were made of. These are traces of an earlier house that used to belong to a noble family, and was purchased by King Władysław Jagiello, who then donated the building to the University. Adjacent buildings were purchased as the university grew, and so the Collegium Maius you see today was created.

Walking along the Collegium Maius wall, turn left into Św. Anny. The next building on your left is the **Collegium Nowodworskie**, Krakow's first grammar school, established in 1588, and now the seat of the Collegium Medicum.

Łaski, a nobleman of decidedly dubious credentials, who conspired tirelessly against King Stefan Batory (*see p. 68*). In addition to holding seances, which had a very unfavourable result for the King - "God" decreed that Batory should cede his crown to Łaski - this magus was also believed to have been spying for Queen Elizabeth I of England. Controversial as he was, John Dee was a learned man, and one of the first advocates of Copernicus' heliocentric theory in

Opposite is St Anne's, **the University Church,** and arguably the most beautiful Baroque building in the city (*see p. 75*). On leaving the church head out to the Planty ring. Turn left and you come to the 19th-century, neo-Gothic **Collegium Novum** building, based on a design by Feliks Księzarski. The façade is adorned with a number of benefactors' coats of arms, as well as that of the University Rector (St. Stanislaus holding a shield with an eagle), as this is where "his Magnificence the Rector" resides. Inside, the massive staircase takes up half the space of the building. Perhaps the most interesting room in the building is the University Aula, where a portrait gallery of famous professors and alumni look on impassively at the open lectures or chamber music concerts held here.

For lunch walk back round to the Collegium Maius in Jagiellońska and try Padva just opposite, perhaps the best Italian restaurant in town, or - for a more economical option - there's the Chimera salad bar in nearby Św. Anny, popular with Jagiellonian University students and their professors.

PART IV

DAY TRIPS

This section offers three trips further afield, beginning with pre-history, moving through the Middle Ages, and ending with a grandiose Socialist Realist experiment. Details of how to get to each of the destinations is included in the text.

Day trip destinations are marked on the regional map on p. 153.

DAY TRIPS

MYSTERIOUS MOUNDS

A perfect destination for a Sunday walk are Krakow's Mounds. Distant relatives of Stonehenge and Newgrange, the Krakus Mound (*Kopiec Krakusa*) and Wanda's Mound (*Kopiec Wandy*), are prehistoric man-made hillocks, about fifty feet high, and almost six miles apart. Like their Irish siblings, they constitute an astronomical calendar of a kind. Looking from the Krakus Mound on the eve of the Celtic festival of the sun, 1st May, you can see the sun rising exactly above Wanda's Mound. Sikornik Hill overlooks the sunrise above the Krakus Mound on the Celtic New Year, 1st November.

According to Krakow's mediæval chronicler Jan Długosz, the mounds were erected to commemorate the first, legendary ruler of Krakow, Krak, from whom the city derives its name. Krak had a daughter, Wanda, whom another legend tells us chose to jump to her death into the Vistula river rather than marry a

The mysterious mounds of Krakow.

foreigner. Later historians and scholars have given various interpretations of the intriguing humps on the skyline: burial sites, fortifications, pagan temples? No one knows.

In the early 19th century, after southern Poland had fallen to the Habsburgs, the people of Krakow erected another mound on Sikornik Hill, to commemorate Tadeusz Kościuszko, who had fought in vain for the freedom of Poland (*see p. 48*). Near Kościuszko's Mound, the fourth hillock, *Kopiec Piłsudskiego*, was erected between 1934 and 1937 to commemorate Marshal Piłsudski, the leader of the revived Polish state (*see p. 48*).

On Sunday afternoons and major holidays you will see a distinctly Cracovian ritual: families complete with grandparents and toddlers, more often than not in their Sunday best, majestically strolling along the path that follows the gentle slope of Sikornik Hill. A slightly fitter pedestrian can take the path further: to Lasek Wolski and the Krakow Zoo, or to Przegorzały, and Bielany Monastery.

To walk up Kościuszko's Mound, take tram number 1, 2 or 6 to Salwator, and walk up Al. Waszyngtona. Turn right at the end of the path - you will see the red brick of the former Austrian fortifications, with the entrance to the Mound.

THE MEDIÆVAL SALT MINE AT WIELICZKA

The ancient salt mine of Wieliczka, over 700 years old, comprises a warren of marvellous underground chambers whose air is famous for its medicinal properties - so take a deep breath. Noted fans of the Wieliczka salt mines have included Polish kings, Nicolas Copernicus, Goethe, Tsar Alexander I, and the Austro-Hungarian Emperor Franz Joseph. To get a flavour - literally - of what excited them so much, why not lick the walls? No one will stop you; it's officially sanctioned.

The salty underground labyrinth stretches and meanders for hundreds of miles. Old maps show 26 shafts starting at the surface, and over 180 smaller underground shafts extending to two or more neighbouring levels. There are nine levels in total, and over 2,000 chambers where excavation has now been abandoned. The route starts at the Daniłowicz Shaft and takes you through a small mile-long stretch of this fascinating underworld, between levels 1 and 3.

According to the chronicles the Wieliczka salt deposits were discovered in the following manner: a 13th-century princess, Kinga, daughter of the

A salty detail in Wieliczka.

Hungarian King Béla IV of the Árpád dynasty, married Bolesław the Bashful, Duke of Krakow and Sandomierz. She brought with her to Poland a large dowry, which helped rebuild the country after much destruction during the Tartar raids. Part of this dowry, apparently, was salt, which in those days was as valuable a commodity as gold. When touring Hungary, Kinga had seen the salt mines of Máramaros, and had asked her father, King Béla, to give her one of the shafts as a present. Her father consented, and Princess Kinga threw her gold ring into the pit, as a way of claiming her possession of it. When salt mines were later founded in Poland, it is said that Kinga showed the miners where to dig. When they unearthed the first nugget of salt, they found the very same ring that she had thrown into the Máramaros shaft embedded inside it.

The Wieliczka tour takes you to chapels carved in salt, to huge, fantastically shaped multi-level chambers, and along salty subterranean lakes that give off eerie reflections of light. Look for the 17th-century chapel of St Anthony, where the saint's expression is softened by the moisture coming through the shaft. The colossal chapel of the Blessed Kinga resembles a church nave hewn out of salt. You will see powerful and ancient timber beams conserved in salt,

1950s Labour Day poster of Nowa Huta.

moss-like saline deposits known as salt flowers, and grandiose chandeliers made entirely of salt-crystals. Lear's Cordelia would have had a field day!

After finishing the tour, you can visit the underground museum, which presents the history of salt mining at Wieliczka, as well as the archaeology and geology of the salty region.

To get to Wieliczka, you can either join one of the organised tours offered at hotels and travel offices, or else go by train or a mini Lux-bus, which leaves every 15 minutes from outside the Main Railway Station. The journey takes around half an hour. Individual visitors or small parties do not need to make a reservation; however, they may be asked to wait up to half an hour for a group to form. Each group is accompanied by a professional guide, usually an ex-miner, who knows his history well, but loves seasoning it with jokes and anecdotes: just take it with a pinch of salt, so to speak. Visitors usually go down the mine on foot (378 steps, or 64 metres), and return by lift, but it is possible to take the lift down for an additional small charge. It is a long walk, so make sure you wear comfortable walking shoes! The temperature in the mine is 14°C all year round. Facilities down the mine include a post office, gift shops, cafés and snack-bars.

In the summer (16th April-15th October), Wieliczka Mine is open daily 7.30am-6.30pm, in winter 8am-4pm. Closed Easter Sunday, 1st November, 4th December, Christmas Eve, Christmas Day and Boxing Day, as well as New Year's Eve and New Year's Day. Reservations for groups can be made by phone on 278-73-02 or 278-73-66.

NOWA HUTA, A BRAVE NEW WORLD

Visiting Nowa Huta involves a tram ride out of the city centre, and then another from its housing estate to the actual foundry. This fascinating 1950s new town is worth the trek, but take tram tickets with you

Take the 4/15 tram from the city centre out east. The journey passes over a weird, scarred industrial landscape dotted with high rises, very different from the housing in central Krakow. Coloured balconies alleviate the grey of the blocks, and the great blue P of a pharmaceutical company lightens one of them on your right, about halfway along the seven-kilometre journey. Get off the tram at plac Centralny. To the south is the low 70s block of the Nowa Huta

Map showing the extent of the Nowa Huta steelworks.

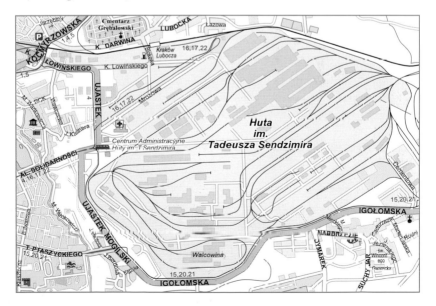

Cultural Centre, with photo, art and sculpture galleries and its fair share of folk dance ensembles, puppet shows and ballets. It looks over a wide view of the valley below and the southernmost suburbs of the city.

The central square was designed by four architects, and construction began in 1949. It relies on traditional town planning models: a central square with residential streets converging into it. The architecture is stark Stalinist neo-Renaissance.

Cracovians say that the model workers' town and steel mill was forced upon them as a way of punishing the city for its conservative tradition and perhaps its reluctance to accept the Communist government in a referendum in 1946. Nowa Huta today is more than just a relic of an experiment gone wrong, however. It still employs about 10,000, a lot given the huge redundancies that have been made over the last decade. The central garden once held a massive statue of Lenin, which some workers attempted to blow up in 1979. But Lenin kept at least one foot on the ground as they only succeeded in destroying one of his legs. Strangely enough he is still standing, in a Swedish amusement park, where he was taken after being torn down by the mob in 1989. Lenin in fact

Lenin standing tall over the Nowa Huta of old.

lived in Krakow in 1912, before the Russian Revolution when he was *persona non grata* in Moscow, and Stalin writes of how he visited him here the following year.

Immediately next to the 50s workers' town is the expanded 70s version. Workers were provided with schools, nurseries and crêches, were set extraordinary 500% norms and were praised as the proletarian vanguard, while the university-educated were also hauled in to do their bit for the revolution.

From plac Centralny you can either take tram 4 back to the city, or trams 4, 16, 17 or 22 to the factory itself. It is only a few stops to the steel mill, and worth the effort for the monumental Joseph S. De Mille set that sits in this otherwise pastoral landscape. The journey takes you past a lake on the left and poor country dwellings in the woods. The main gate of the factory looms gigantic in this rural setting. It is known locally as the "Doge's Palace", and one can quite see why. Venetian palaces of dubious aspect guard the entrance to this huge complex with its gigantic steel sign before it.

In August 2001, film director Andrzej Wajda set up a temporary Museum of Socialist Realism, with plans for a permanent show from July 2002. You can take a bus tour of the steelworks itself. A minimum of 20 people are needed per tour, and booking must be made at least two weeks in advance. Either book at PTTK, Stalowa 15, in Nowa Huta itself, or ring 643 7905. Visiting hours are between 9am and 3pm.

A recent theme of the Krakow International Architectural Bi-annual Competition was "More geometry, less ideology". Architects from all over the world were invited to submit plans for the future of Nowa Huta. Let's hope that, like the new factory management, they can turn the place around and make this brave new world a going concern.

PART V

PRACTICALITIES

FOOD & DRINK

King Zygmunt Vasa may have transferred the royal court from Krakow to Warsaw in 1609, but Krakow nevertheless remained a capital for Poland's culture and learning, not to mention its culinary life. This last accolade has been reaffirmed in recent years, when the Poles' famous love of a good night out has had the freedom to return. Most the restaurants popular today have materialised over the last twelve years, while some ancient, battered establishments have undergone a thorough overhaul.

Cracovians take their food seriously. The city even boasts the Galician Gourmet Academy, composed of Cracovian gourmets, artists and intellectuals. Every year, they convene in Noworolski Café on the Rynek and elect the winner of the *Złota Kawka* (the Golden Jackdaw) Prize, awarded to the best restaurant in town. The list of laureates includes Cyrano de Bergerac, Nowina, Pod Różą, La Fontaine, and Copernicus (*see below*).

Obwarzanki or plaited Polish bread rolls.

Hot summers and freezing winters mean that Krakow's restaurant culture is highly climate-conscious. In the summer, the streets of Krakow carry a palpable hint of the Mediterranean. When winter comes, Cracovians seek the fireside warmth of bars and restaurants snugly situated in mediæval chambers and cellars. There is nothing like a hearty Polish meal when you want to get warm and make friends with the winter.

The stereotypical Polish menu is a depressingly monotonous cavalcade of pork, potatoes and cabbage. If anywhere is going to break that mould, it's Krakow. Not that you can't find the heavy and wholesome traditional fare - you can. And a lot of local dishes are something of an acquired taste, for example *żurek* (soup made from a base of fermented rye flour) or beetroot *barszcz* (borscht). But people of so many different nationalities and traditions have left their mark on Krakow's architecture and language, that inevitably their inheritance can be traced in the cuisine as well. Dishes now considered typically Polish are often a mixture of Russian, German, Ukrainian, Italian, Jewish, Lithuanian, Turkish, French and other recipes, brought to Krakow, and happily assimilated, with an added pinch of the famous *genius loci*.

POPULAR STARTERS

Befsztyk tatarski, or *tatar* (beef tartare): made from "scraped" (rather than minced or chopped) raw beef sirloin.

Talerz wędlin (a cold meat platter): This should include tender cured ham, and *kiełbasa* (sausage), preferably *lisiecka*, made in a village of Liszki near Krakow.

Grilled *oscypek*: (sheep's cheese from the Tatra Mountains).

Smalec (dripping): served with bacon crackling and herbs, it goes well with hearty Polish bread.

Węgorz wędzony (smoked eel), and *pasztet z zająca* (wild hare pâté) are two other savoury staples.

CHEESE

A dispute rages over two traditional cheeses, *oscypek* (or *oszczypek*) and *bunc* (*bundz*). *Oscypek* is a mature, hard cheese, often smoked, in the characteristic shape of two cones joined at their base. The softer, white and compact *bunc* is similar in consistency to mozzarella; after a second maturation, *bunc* becomes

salty and spicy *bryndza*. Both are very traditional mountain cheeses, and work is afoot to introduce an *appellation controlée* - the only problem being that no one can agree what the terms of it should be. The sooner it comes in the better, though, as there are some sad excuses for *oscypek* around, including most of those sold by "authentic mountaineers" in the streets of Krakow. You have been warned! If you want the real thing, look in Pod Aniołami, next to the restaurant of the same name at Grodzka No. 35. The shop also sells wonderful square loaves of dark bread (*ciemny chleb*) and smaller, rounder, white *kukułki*.

SOUPS

Perhaps the most typical Polish soup is *barszcz czerwony* (red borscht), a beetroot broth that can be served clear (*barszcz czysty*), or with tiny ravioli filled with meat (*uszka z mięsem*) or, even better, forest mushrooms (*uszka z grzybami*). Red borscht with mushroom-filled ravioli is a part of traditional Christmas Eve dinner. *Barszcz* goes well also with a hot pastry filled with meat (*barszcz z*

Liszki sausage.

pasztecikiem; or *barszcz z krokietem*) or cabbage (*barszcz z kapuśniaczkiem*). The stock for borscht is made either of meat or mushrooms; the soup base, made of beetroot and other vegetables and herbs has to be marinated for about a week. Proper *barszcz* is a very noble and elegant soup indeed.

Another wonderful sour soup is *żurek*, sometimes called *barszcz biały* (white borscht). The soup base is made from fermented rye flour, garlic, herbs, and wholemeal bread. *Żurek* is often served with boiled white sausage (*biała kiełbasa*) and/or hard-boiled egg and potatoes, although there are other variations as well. *Żurek* is known for its restorative effects on hangover sufferers. Other popular soups are *rosół* (chicken or beef bouillon), the eternal soup of Polish Sunday lunch, most often served with noodles (*z makaronem*), and *pomidorowa* (tomato soup), sometimes accompanied with rice (*z ryżem*), and often thickened with sour cream. Typical wholesome wintertime soups include *krupnik*, a thick barley soup with a variety of vegetables and chunks of meat, and *kapuśniak* – sauerkraut soup with potatoes, while mushroom soup served in bread (*zupa grzybowa w chlebie*) is delicious all year round. *Chłodnik* is a cold soup, served in the summer only. The most commonly found is *chłodnik*

Oscypek mountain sheep's cheese.

litewski (Lithuanian style *chłodnik*) made of beetroot, but some cold fruit soups, for example raspberry (*chłodnik malinowy*) or strawberry (*chłodnik truskawkowy*), made from fresh fruit, and not at all sweet or cloying, flash through the menus now and then, like comets. *Zupa ogórkowa* (cucumber soup), though served warm, can also be refreshing.

MAIN COURSES

Maczanka po Krakowsku: pork stewed with onion and caraway, and served in a sauce-drenched bread-roll.

Gołąbki (literally "little pigeons"): cabbage leaves stuffed with rice and meat, served with a tomato or mushroom cream sauce.

Bigos: a stew made of fresh cabbage and sauerkraut, prunes, bacon, sausage, herbs, and spices. It is one of those rare and ancient dishes that get better day after day as you reheat them.

Pierogi: boiled dumplings with different kinds of fillings: *pierogi ruskie* (Russian *pierogi*) have potato, curd cheese and onion; *pierogi z mięsem* have meat. There are sweet *pierogi* variations as well. The filling for *pierogi leniwe* (literally "lazy" *pierogi*) is made of sweet curd cheese, and there are fruit fillings in the summer too: the unbeatable *pierogi z jagodami* (fresh blueberries), *pierogi z truskawkami* (strawberries), or *pierogi z wiśniami* (cherries).

Of the most typical meat dishes, look for *schab ze śliwkami* (roast pork with prunes), *kaczka pieczona* (roast duck, often served with baked apples and potatoes), *zrazy zawijane z kaszą gryczaną* (a rolled slice of beef sirloin filled with smoked bacon and pickled cucumber, served with buckwheat), *pieczone prosię* (roast suckling pig), *żeberka* (spare-ribs), and *golonko* (surprisingly tasty, considering they are pig's trotters, often served complete with skin, bristles and all). Cracovian *sznycel* is not the same as Wiener Schnitzel – the latter is *kotlet schabowy* (pork or veal cutlet), while *sznycel* is the poorer version of the dish, made of minced meat.

To accompany your main course you can choose a *sałatka* or *surówka*, for instance the unrivalled *buraczki* - or *ćwikła z chrzanem* – boiled or lightly pickled beetroot, often with horseradish. Main courses are most commonly accompanied by potatoes (*ziemniaki*) in different styles, but look out for *kasza gryczana* (buckwheat) as well.

PUDDINGS

Traditional sweets include *pączki* (doughnuts, full and round, often filled with wild rosehip jam), *nugat* (nougat, two wafers with very sweet filling made from honey, nuts, and egg yolks), *piszinger* (many layers of wafer with chocolate filling), *szarlotka* (apple pie), *sernik* (cheese-cake), or *cwibak* (baked cake with nuts and dried fruit).

RESTAURANTS

International influence has entered the Cracovian culinary scene. The last twelve years have witnessed the arrival of French, Italian, Japanese, Chinese, Indian, Greek, Mexican and Ukrainian chefs. Below is a wholly personal and selective list of the best restaurants in town.

Price of an average 3-course meal for one (excluding drinks):
$ Cheap: around 50-60 złoty (12-15 US$);
$$ Moderate: up to 100 złoty (25 US$);
$$$ Expensive: 100 złoty and over.

Restaurants are all in the Old Town (Stare Miasto) unless otherwise stated.

POLISH & CENTRAL EUROPEAN

C.K. DEZERTER
Bracka 6. Tel: 422-79-31. 9am-11pm; Fri and Sat till midnight; Sun 10.00-23.00. $
Solid and inexpensive Austro-Hungarian fare - with Emperor Franz Joseph watching over you as you eat. Good traditional dishes such as *pierogi*, grilled *oscypek* cheese, or spare ribs in honey sauce. Excellent micro-brew too.

CHIMERA
Św. Anny 3. Tel: 423-21-78. Noon-10pm. $$
Game and poultry dishes, good soups and desserts. The restaurant shares vast cellars with a popular and inexpensive salad bar.

CHŁOPSKIE JADŁO

Św. Agnieszki 1 (Under Wawel). Tel: 421-85-20. Noon-10pm; Fri and Sat noon-midnight. Also at Św. Jana 3. Tel: 429-51-57. Noon-11pm. $$

Literally "peasants' food", Chłopskie Jadło is decorated to look like a traditional cottage, and serves typical Polish dishes. For larger groups, *niecka* is a good option - a selection of various Polish specialities. Live folk music Thur, Fri, Sat pm.

COPERNICUS

Kanonicza 16. Tel: 431-10-44. Noon till late. $$$

Elegant and imaginative menu with Polish influences. In ul. Kanonicza, one of Krakow's loveliest corners, at the foot of Wawel Hill. Expensive, but worth every złoty. Winner of the 2001 "Golden Jackdaw" Prize for the best restaurant in Krakow.

JAREMA

Plac Matejki 5 (Kleparz). Tel: 429-36-69. Noon till late. $$

Polish-Lithuanian classics, or culinary nostalgia for the former borderland. Winner of the "Golden Jackdaw's Egg" for the best *pierogi* in town.

POD ANIOŁAMI

Grodzka 35. Tel: 421-39-99. 1pm-

Poselska, the street of restaurants.

midnight; Fri and Sat till 1 am. $$
Good Polish classics. Cosy cellar
with fireplace, wood, tapestries and
the angels that the name of the
restaurant promises. Excellent
grilled *oscypek*, meat and poultry.

POD BARANEM
Św. Gertrudy 21. Tel: 429-40-22.
11am-10pm; Sun and holidays till
10pm. $
Some of the best Polish recipes, from
popular dishes to rare classics, such
as game, freshwater fish, and wild
mushrooms.

TETMAJEROWSKA
Rynek Główny 34. Tel: 422-06-31.
1.30pm till late. $$$
Elegant restaurant boasting a frieze

by Włodzimierz Tetmajer and black
caviar from the restaurant's own
fish-farms in Siberia.

INTERNATIONAL

A LA CARTE
Izaaka 7 (Kazimierz). Tel: 430-65-50.
Noon-midnight. $$$
A tiny restaurant with a sophis-
ticated menu (mainly French-
inspired, with some touches of
Oriental) and décor to match (a
goldfish bowl at every table, slightly
disconcerting when you order trout
or sturgeon).

METROPOLITAN
Sławkowska 3. Tel: 421-98-03.
8.30am-midnight; Sun till 10pm. $$

Pierogi dumplings, classic Polish fare.

Cosmopolitan, with a drift towards the Mediterranean.

ORIENT EXPRESS
Poselska 22. Tel: 422-66-72. Noon-11pm. $
Lovely luxurious train compartments on this journey. Great menu includes such classics as French pastries, Italian pastas, and Hungarian "Gundel" pancake (chocolate and walnut filling) for dessert.

POD RÓŻĄ
Floriańska 14. Tel: 422-12-44. Noon-11pm; closed between 3.30pm-6.30pm. $$$
Built in the converted courtyard of a tenement house, Pod Różą restaurant feels airy and spacious under its glass roof. Pleasant and light in both the décor and the menu. Impeccable service.

WENTZL
Rynek Główny 19. Tel: 429-57-12. 1pm-midnight. $$$
Innovative cuisine with bold - not necessarily beautiful - interior décor. Outdoor garden in summer.

JEWISH (NON-KOSHER)

ALEF
Szeroka 17 (Kazimierz). Tel: 421-38-70. 9am till late. $

A cosy interior with Klezmer music played on most nights (the ticket is charged to your bill). Jewish themes appear both in the décor and on the menu.

KLEZMER HOIS
Szeroka 6 (Kazimierz). Tel: 411-12-45. 7am till late.
Jewish-style fare in a cosy, homely interior. Klezmer music concerts in the evenings.

MEDITERRANEAN

AMARONE
Floriańska 14. Tel: 429-15-23. Noon-11pm. $$
Italian restaurant - sister of the more cosmopolitan Pod Różą - and sharing the same building. Italian wine cellar.

AVANTI
Karmelicka 7 (Piasek). Tel: 430-07-70. 1pm-11pm. $
Reliable Italian restaurant, near the Planty - the green ring which marks the border of the Old Town.

CARUSO
Grodzka 39. Tel: 422-60-61. Noon till midnight. $
Elegant Italian cuisine, with pastas freshly made by the chef, a native of Naples.

CHERUBINO
Św. Tomasza 15. Tel: 429-40-07.
Mon-Sat noon till midnight; Sun till
11pm. $
An easy-going, popular restaurant serving both Italian and traditional Polish dishes. Atmospherically lit, and filled with patinated antiques and magic vehicles, such as a winged wooden sledge, and a flying boat.

CORLEONE
Poselska 19. Tel: 429-51-26. Noon-
midnight. $
Decent Italian menu with a "rustic Sicilian" interior, decorated with Fellini film stills.

CYRANO DE BERGERAC
Sławkowska 26. Tel: 411-72-88. Mon-
Sat noon-midnight. Closed Sun and
holidays. $$$
A reliable French restaurant in a mediæval cellar.

GULIWER
Bracka 6. Tel: 422-79-31. 9am-11pm;
Fri and Sat till midnight; Sun 10am-
11pm. $
Interior of a French inn, food simple yet tasty. One of Czesław Miłosz's favourite restaurants.

LA FONTAINE
Sławkowska 1. Tel: 431-09-30. Noon-
late (kitchen closes 11pm). $$$
Owner-chef Pierre Gaillard, a disciple of Paul Bocusse, is a true artist and his dishes little works of art. He brings some Polish notes to his creations.

PADVA
*Jagiellońska. Tel: 292-02-72. Open
noon-midnight. $$$*
Italian restaurant right opposite
Collegium Maius.

PAESE
*Poselska 24. Tel: 421-62-73. Noon-
late. $$*
Rustic and cosy interior, the only
Corsican restaurant in Poland. Good
soups and fish dishes, but best of all,

Calvi: tender sirloin steak in
Roquefort sauce.

ORIENTAL

A DONG
*Brodzińskiego 3 (Podgórze). Tel: 656-
48-72. 11am-11pm. $.*
The best Chinese-Vietnamese restaurant in town; slightly out of the way,
on the other side of the river, in
Podgórze.

CAFÉS & BARS

Most Cracovians would not survive without them. What else could sustain
"café philosophers", "café politicians", and "café artists"? How many theories
would stay un-formed, poems un-written, songs un-composed, improvements
un-planned? Where would readers of books sip and savour the true taste of the
city?

The first café known to appear in Krakow was established around 1775 in
the Rynek at No. 31, though the business as such only started to flourish when
pastry-cooks entered the scene, and Krakow discovered its sweet tooth. As a
café philosopher would put it, there is nothing like a coffee and a cake to rec-
oncile you to the essential duality of life, to enjoy its bittersweet taste. Many of
Krakow's cafés offer a small selection of home-made cakes. The biggest café in
Krakow is the mediæval Rynek, THE square. The moment it fills with café
tables and parasols, it is a sure sign that spring has arrived. This, the biggest
open-air café in town, stays open well into October, sometimes November if
weather allows. Rynek's "garden cafés" are a favourite place for both locals and
visitors to sip a beer or a coffee, watch the life of the city pass by, and tune in
to its different sounds: birds, buskers, orchestras, and the *hejnał*, the ancient
bugle-call played from the tower of St. Mary's (*see p. 35*), which marks each

passing hour. There are well over a dozen cafés all around the Rynek, including: Bankowa, Pod Słońcem, Loża, Redolfi, Europejska, Bambus, Café Sukiennice, Arlekin, Pod Baranami, Szara and Noworolski. pick your favourite spot!

NB: All cafés are in the Old Town (Stare Miasto) unless otherwise stated.

ALCHEMIA
Kazimierz, Estery 5.
They say that Alchemia was once an alchemist's laboratory. Now a cross between a café and a bar, with an alchemical theme, it is so popular that weekdays are often more magical than weekends. Apple pie is what most alchemists go for.

BOTANICA
Bracka 9.
A student favourite with a wintergarden full of potted plants. Good for coffee and a light snack.

CAMELOT
Św. Tomasza 17.
Arty crowd that likes the stylish interior, good salads and British and American newspapers. With a selection of naive art works and a refusal to sell Coca-Cola or Pepsi.

DEMMERS TEEHAUS
Kanonicza 21.
For connoisseurs of tea from every which where.

DYM
Św. Tomasza 13.
With works by local photographers on show, try its renowned wafer and chocolate *piszinger* and cheese-cake. The name means "smoke", and it certainly lives up to it.

JAMA MICHALIKA
Floriańska 45.
The most famous confectionery-café in Krakow, established in 1895. The interior, designed by Karol Frycz, is filled with enormous armchairs, organic mouldings and murals, stained-glass windows and oval mirrors. The shapes and forms of the furniture perhaps look to Charles Rennie Mackintosh as a possible influence. Opinion is divided as to whether the original owner of the café, Jan Michalik, who came to Krakow from Lviv (Lemberg in those days, and capital of Galicia, the Austrian-ruled province of Poland), was a clever and thrifty merchant, or a generous patron of the arts, who accepted drawings and paintings in

lieu of payment, and bonded with the bohemians over late-night vodkas, after the place had officially closed.

Among the multitude of ornaments and icons is a satirical "Japanese" painting, complete with inlaid *kanji* inscription, of the eccentric art collector Feliks Jasieński, clad in his famous black cloak, under which he is said to have smuggled paintings he liked out of his artist friends' studios. Here he is flying to Japan with the artist Leon Wyczółkowski. Jasieński's weakness for things Oriental produced a unique collection, which you can now see in Krakow's Japanese Museum – Manggha (*see p. 52*).

KRZYSZTOFORY
Szczepańska 2.
Next to the palace of the same name, this is a café-cum-gallery. Service can be relaxed, but the artworks are usually worth a look.

Noworolski Café in the Sukiennice.

Cheese-cake and apple pie.

LAROUSSE
Św. Tomasza 22.
A tiny place (teeny-tiny - a mere three tables) decorated with the pages from guess which French dictionary?

NOWOROLSKI
Rynek Główny 1 (in the Sukiennice).
Atmospheric turn-of-the-century décor - and turn-of-the-century clientèle, too. Redolent of faded elegance, and with one of the best views anywhere in town.

POŚEGNANIE Z AFRYKĄ (Out of Africa)
Św. Tomasza 21.
One of the few non-smoking cafete-rias in Krakow, serving gourmet coffees from all over the world. Just name your bean - they've got it. There is also an adjoining shop selling bags of fragrant coffee.

PROPAGANDA
Kazimierz, Miodowa 20.
A little museum of Communist memorabilia. Salute Stalin and other heroes of Socialist Realism as you down your drink.

RIO
Św. Jana 2.
Established in 1946, then remodelled in 1961, it has not really changed since then. This is real retroland, beloved by dotty professors.

Bars

In bars and in some cafés the selection of vodkas is impressive; and if you are not a connoisseur of clear vodka, consumed ice-cold, there is a selection of flavoured vodkas and interesting cocktails.

One of the most popular cocktails is *Teraz Polska*, or Poland Now, which is the name of a competition for the best Polish product; the winners can use the red-and-white logo of a stylised Polish flag. The cocktail, also known as *flagowiec* (the flagship), consists of thick red pomegranate juice with pure white vodka poured slowly on top of it.

Żubrówka, or bison vodka, is flavoured with the grass from the Białowieża virgin forest on which the bison feed (a tipsy Pole will tell you that they do not only FEED on the grass). It has a yellowish-green tint and a matching, subtly herbal flavour. It goes very well with apple juice; the mixture is called *szarlotka* (apple pie) or *tatanka*. *Dzięgielówka*, made from angelica root, has a light flavour. *Piołunówka*, made with wormwood, kicks like a mule. *Wiśniówka* is a sweet cherry vodka, and *krupnik* is a sweetish spirit made from honey. Flavoured vodkas should not be chilled lest they lose their flavour. In the winter, there is nothing better than *gorący miód* (hot mead), *grzaniec galicyjski* (mulled wine with spices) or a *krupnik* vodka with hot water and lemon.

In the summer, cold beer will revive you. Polish beer, almost exclusively synonymous with lager, is quite good, although take-overs of local breweries by big multinationals have shaken the quality of production for some time. The brands of Żywiec, Okocim, or Leżajsk may be difficult to pronounce, but the word for beer - *piwo* (pronounced: "pivo") - is refreshingly simple.

Many of Krakow's watering holes live double lives: cafés during the day, they become bars at night.

NB: *All bars are in the Old Town (Stare Miasto) unless otherwise stated.*

Black Gallery
Mikołajska 24.
Try a kamikaze or scorpion vodka cocktail here, served on plates full of little shot glasses. In summer their courtyard is one of the coolest spots in town.

Klub Kulturalny
Szewska 25.
Famous for its mosaic floor, and very popular with academics shaking away the cobwebs. Locals know it as "Ko-Ko". Open late.

Improve your French in the Larousse Café in Św. Tomasza.

PAPARAZZI
Mikołajska 9.
Snaps of the famous as the name suggests. This place really knows how to mix a cocktail. English-speaking staff.

SINGER
Kazimierz, Estery 20.
Sit and pedal the eponymous sewing machines in time to the sounds of Piaf or Brel. Candlelit penumbra suits the mood of the would-be poets who throng to this place.

STALOWE MAGNOLIE
Św. Jana 15.
Jazz, rock and blues club with a tough door policy (dress smart and ring the buzzer if you don't have a club card). The music is excellent and the cocktail list will spoil you for choice.

TAM I Z POWROTEM (There and back again)
Kazimierz, Pl. Nowy.
A wide variety of beers, both bottled and on tap, and good bar food.

HOTELS
& ACCOMMODATION

There are some excellent hotels in Krakow - but they tend to be expensive. Charming, central hotels at a reasonable price are still rare. Here is a selective list of some of the best hotels in their price ranges. Prices quoted (in dollars or Euros) are for a double room. It may be worth ringing round for special offers, or searching on the Internet to get better rates. *www.visiblecities.net* maintains a list of hotels with updates and readers' comments.

COPERNICUS****
Kanonicza 16. Tel: (48-12) 424-34-00
Fax: (48-12) 424-34-05
www.hotel.com.pl
29 rooms, 8 suites
Restaurant, café, bar. Swimming pool, sauna and fitness club included in the price.
$185-210

In a renovated mediæval house in arguably the most magical and certainly the oldest street in Krakow, Kanonicza. A story goes that Copernicus himself once stayed here. Traces of history remain in Renaissance portals, wall paintings and floor mosaics. All rooms are air-conditioned, with mini-bar, TV and jacuzzi. Most have Internet access.

POD RÓŻĄ***
Floriańska 14. Tel: (48-12) 424-33-00
Fax: (48-12) 424-33-51
www.hotel.com.pl
54 rooms, 3 suites
2 restaurants, wine cellar.
$140

Located in the "Royal Tract", leading from St Florian's mediæval city gate to Wawel Hill, now a busy and fashionable shopping street. Pod Różą was an inn in the 18th century, although the building itself is four centuries older. Recently renovated, it is comfortable and elegant. The inner courtyard, covered with a glass roof, now houses one of the finest restaurants in Krakow.

GRAND**
Sławkowska 5-7. Tel: (48 12) 421-72-55
Fax: (48 12) 421-83-60
www.grand.pl
50 rooms, 6 suites
Restaurant, bar, café.
$189

One of the oldest hotels in Krakow, close to the Rynek. The former Czartoryski Palace, it became a hotel in 1885. Elegant and comfortable.

FRANCUSKI**
Pijarska 13. Tel: (48 12) 422-51-22
Fax: (48 12) 422-52-70
www.orbis.pl/hot_fra.html
27 rooms, 15 suites
Restaurant, bar.
€171

"The French Hotel" is just across the street from the Czartoryski Museum, home to Leonardo Da Vinci's *Lady with an Ermine*. The hotel boasts an impressive staircase, and stylish interiors with a fin-de-siècle feel.

CRACOVIA**
Focha 1. Tel: (48-12) 422-86-66
Fax: (48-12) 421-95-86
www.orbis.pl/polish/hot_cra_p.html
235 rooms, 9 suites
Restaurant, café.
€135

One of the largest hotels in Krakow, this hotel is a typical three-star standard. Very close to the Błonia - the largest green space in the city. It is also across the street from the New Building of the National Museum, and within the walking distance from the town centre.

AMADEUS****

Mikołajska 20. Tel: (48 12) 429-60-70
Fax: (48 12) 429-60-62
www.hotel-amadeus.pl
20 rooms, 2 suites
Restaurant, café, bar.
$160

A stone's throw from the Rynek, this small hotel is one of Krakow's newest. In style and ambience, it claims the Rococo world of Mozart as its inspiration.

WIT STWOSZ***

Mikołajska 28. Tel: (48 12) 429-60-42
Fax (18 12) 429-61-39
www.wit-stwosz.hotel.krakow.pl
17 rooms
Restaurant.
$100

In the Old Town centre, this new hotel aims to combine historical 16th century interiors with contemporary comfort.

POLLERA**

Szpitalna 30. Tel: (48 12) 422-10-44
Fax: (48 12) 422-13-89
www.pollera.com.pl
37 rooms, 2 suites
Restaurant.
€93

Simple rooms that vary in standard and décor. A friendly hotel, within the mediæval city walls, across the street from the Słowackiego Theatre.

SASKI **

Sławowska 3. Tel/Fax: (48 12) 421-42-22; www.hotelsaski.com.pl
60 rooms, 11 suites.
$100

Old-fashioned Central European charm in the centre of the Old Town. Beautiful antique lift. Good location.

DOM GOSCINNY

Floriańska 49. Tel: (48 12) 429-15-68;
Fax: (48 12) 421-12-25.
$85

A Jagiellonian University guesthouse, in a good location. University guests have priority, but you might be lucky.

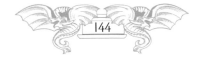
PRACTICAL TIPS

PUBLIC TRANSPORT

Krakow's transport system consists of trains and buses, which are frequent, convenient, and inexpensive. Regular lines run between 5am-11pm, and afterwards night services are available. Season tickets are available for periods of one week to one month. MPK offers daily and weekly passes.

DRIVING

There are traffic restrictions in the city centre, with many pedestrian and semi-pedestrian zones in the Old Town. Only special permits allow you to drive in inner zones. Parking within these designated zones requires a special ticket (*karta postojowa*) which can be bought from a Ruch kiosk. You mark the date and time, and display it in your windscreen.

TAXIS

It is cheaper to take a taxi belonging to a radio taxi company, recognisable by a colourful sign, usually with a four-digit phone number starting with 96 or 919. Private taxis can be much more expensive. Phone rates are cheaper than street rates. Ask a taxi driver for *abonament* or *karta stałego klienta* - a free card which entitles you to the same discount when you take a taxi from the taxi rank as when you order it by phone. Reputable companies include Mega Taxi (9625), Taxi Barbakan (9661), Taxi Partner (9633).

CULTURAL EVENTS & TOURIST INFORMATION

Information about what's on in town is available from the following sources:

TOURIST INFORMATION CENTRE
Rynek Główny, Sukiennice 1/3.
Tel: 421-77-06, 421-30-51.
Mon-Fri 9am-6pm; Sat 9am-2pm (may vary according to demand).

TOURIST INFORMATION POINT
Planty, between the Main Railway Station and Słowackiego Theatre, Szpitalna 25.
Tel: 432-01-10, 432-00-60.
Mon-Fri 8am-8pm; Sat-Sun 9am-5pm.

CULTURAL INFORMATION CENTRE
Św. Jana 2.
Tel: 421-77-87.
www.karnet.krakow2000.pl
Mon-Fri 10am-6pm; Sat 10am-4pm.

TELEPHONE & POSTAL SERVICES

There are plenty of public telephones operated with magnetic cards (*karty telefoniczne*) which can be purchased from post offices or from kiosks. The post offices with the longest opening hours (including some 24-hour sections) are the Main Post Office (*Poczta Główna*) at Westerplatte 20, and the post office at the main railway station. Telekomunikacja Polska has a service point at Rynek Główny 19, where you can phone or send a fax any time between 8am and 10pm. The international code for Poland is 48, the area code for Krakow is 12. For international calls, dial two zeros followed by the country code. Long-distance inside Poland requires 0+10+33 or 44 (two different operating companies) +22+the phone number.

CHANGING MONEY

You can change money in banks or *kantor* offices - the latter offer better rates and are absolutely safe. Travellers cheques can be cashed in some banks. The largest concentration of banks and *kantors*, as well as ATMs, is in the Old Town.

OPENING TIMES

Most shops in the Old Town are open between 10am and 5pm, or 11am and 6pm (some even longer than that). There are several convenience stores open 24 hours a day, 7 days a week (e.g. in Starowiślna, opposite the Main Post Office, or in Basztowa, opposite the LOT building). Sukiennice souvenir stalls in the Rynek are open till dark. Most banks are open between 9am and 5pm (some until 6pm).

Most museums are shut on Mondays, but several close on Tuesdays or Sundays instead (see the Museum section for details).

CLIMATE

The seasons are clearly demarcated. Spring begins in March, cold and windy at first, but gradually getting warmer and sunnier. Summer starts in June, is mainly pleasant and sunny, though it can get very hot, and is sometimes punctuated by short, heavy rainstorms. Autumn comes in September, though October usually offers a last warm burst - *Babie Lato*, the Polish Indian Summer, before November brings the cold, damp and fog, and winter begins in earnest. January and February are the coldest months, and Krakow can usually expect to get a smattering of snow. Average temperatures: 4°C in February, and 27°C in July, though it can go above 30°C in summer, and during the worst of the winter can snap to -20°C - or even lower.

INDEX

Numbers in italics refer to illustrations. Numbers in bold are major references.

Map of Krakow & Environs, Showing Places Mentioned in the Day Trips Section

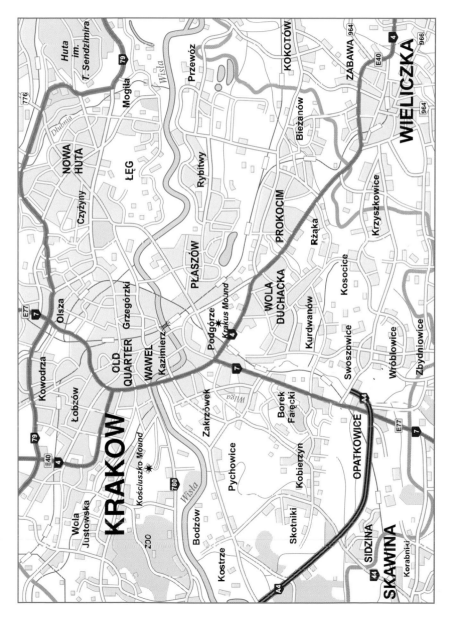

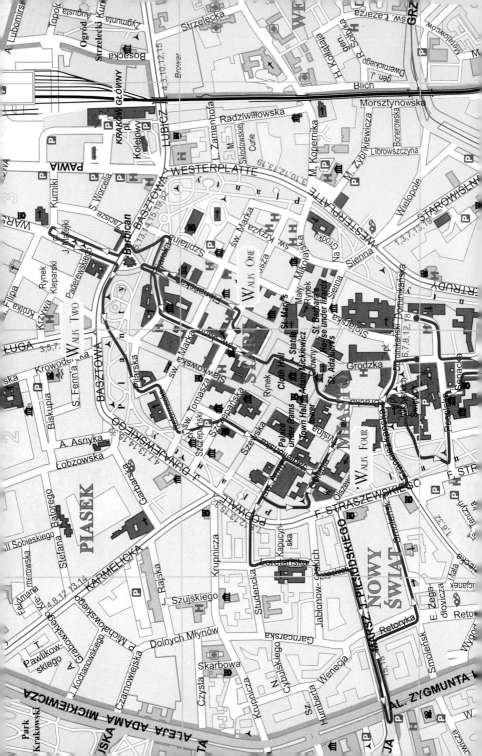

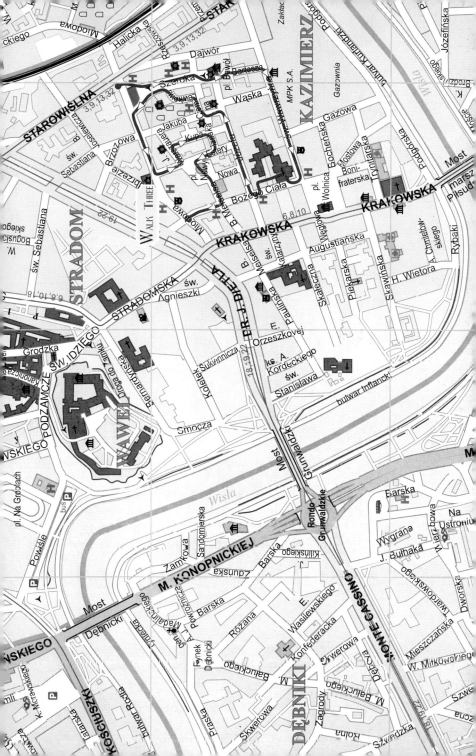

MAP REFERENCES FOR CENTRAL KRAKOW MAP

SIGHTS & MONUMENTS

Barbican A3
Czynciel's House B2
Grunwald Monument A3
Mickiewicz Statue B2
Rynek B2
St Florian's Gate A3
Town Hall Tower B2
Wawel Castle C2
Wawel Hill C2

CHURCHES & SYNAGOGUES

Capuchin Monastery B2
Corpus Christi D3
Dominican B3
Franciscan B2
Isaac's D3
Kupa D3
Old Synagogue D4
Piarist A3
Popper D4
Remuh D3
Skałka D2
St Adalbert B2
St Andrew C2
St Anne B2
St Florian A3
St Katherine D3
St Kazimierz A2
St Mary B2-B3
SS.Peter & Paul C2
Tempel C3

MUSEUMS

Archaeological C2
Archidiocesal C2
Bunker of Art B2
Cricoteka C2
Czartoryski A3
Ethnographic D3
Krakow Historical B2
Jagiellonian University B2
Manggha Centre D2
Matejko B3
Municipal Engineering D4
National Museum, Main
Building B1
Palace of Art B2
Pharmacy B3
Pharmacy (in Podgórze) E4
Sukiennice Painting Gallery
B2
Wyspiański C2

PUBLIC BUILDINGS

Academy of Fine Art A3
Chamber of Commerce A2
Collegium Iuridicum C2
Collegium Kołłątaja B2
Collegium Maius B2
Collegium Minus B2
Collegium Novum B2
Collegium Opolskie B2
District Savings Society A1-
B1
Jagiellonian Library B1
Jewish Cultural Center D3
Kijów Cinema C1
Medical Society B3

Music Academy A2
Palace of Art B2
Philharmonic Hall B2
Press Palace B3
School of Industry B1
Słowackiego Theatre B3
Stary Teatr B2
University of Economics A4

RESTAURANTS, CAFÉS & HOTELS

A Dong A3
A la Carte D3
Alchemia D3
Alef D4
Amadeus Hotel B3
Amarone B3
Avanti B2
Black Gallery B3
Botanica B2
C.K. Dezerter B2
Camelot B2
Caruso C2
Cherubino B2
Chimera B2
Chłopskie Jadło D2
Copernicus C2
Copernicus Hotel &
Restaurant C2
Corleone C2
Cracovia Hotel B1
Cyrano de Bergerac A2
Demmers Teehaus C2
Dom Goscinny B3
Dym B2
Francuski A3

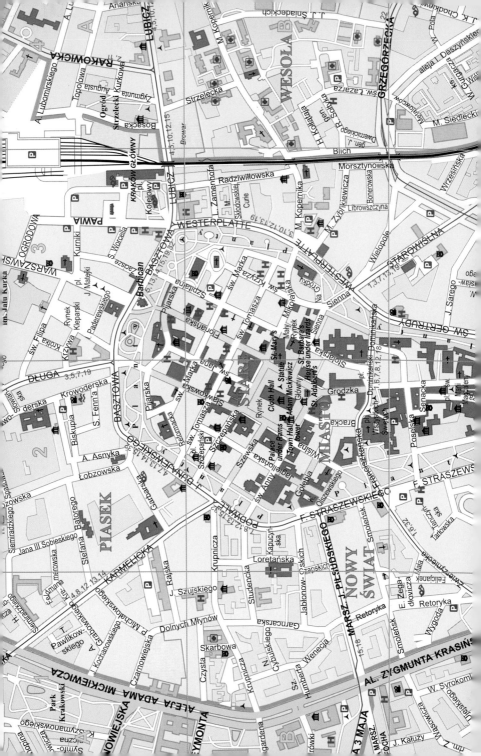